PRIMARY GREATNESS

THE 12 LEVERS OF SUCCESS

STEPHEN R. COVEY

SIMON & SCHUSTER

New York   London   Toronto   Sydney   New Delhi

Simon & Schuster
1230 Avenue of the Americas
New York, NY 10020

First Simon & Schuster hardcover edition November 2015

SIMON & SCHUSTER and colophon are
registered trademarks of Simon & Schuster, Inc.

For information about special discounts for bulk purchases,
please contact Simon & Schuster Special Sales at
1-866-506-1949 or business@simonandschuster.com.

The Simon & Schuster Speakers Bureau can bring authors
to your live event. For more information or to book an event,
contact the Simon & Schuster Speakers Bureau at
1-866-248-3049 or visit our website at www.simonspeakers.com.

Interior design by Claudia Martinez

Manufactured in the United States of America

1 3 5 7 9 10 8 6 4 2

Library of Congress Cataloging-in-Publication Data is available.

ISBN 978-1-5011-0657-6
ISBN 978-1-5011-0695-8 (ebook)

CONTENTS

I

How to Achieve Primary Greatness

II

12 Levers of Success

FOREWORD BY SEAN COVEY

As a young man, my father, Stephen R. Covey, had a job lined up. His father owned a successful hotel chain, and as the oldest son he was set to take over the business.

But a stint as a teacher infected him with a desire to use his talents elsewhere. His own voice—a combination of passion, talent, and conscience—cried out to be heard. He decided he wanted to be a teacher above all else. He had sensed the wondrous potential of his students and burned with a desire to unleash that potential. But he knew his father wanted him to take over the family business. He decided to talk with his father, but he was so afraid of what his father might think.

One day he approached his father and told him he wanted to be a teacher. His father replied, "That's fine, son. You'll be a great teacher. To be honest, I never liked business that much myself." So Dr. Covey went on to become a university professor, a writer, and ultimately one of the world's most sought-after thought leaders on the topics of leadership, organizational effectiveness, and family, all because he had the courage to find his own voice and make a distinctive contribution.

He helped others find their voice too. On one occasion I asked my father what he thought a good definition of leadership was. He said, "Leadership is communicating to another person their worth and potential so clearly they are inspired to see it in themselves."

This was the first time I'd ever heard such a definition, and I teared up a little. Why? Because that definition personified him. He was always communicating to me my worth and potential, even when I didn't see it in myself. He made me feel like I could do anything and that I had an important mission to fulfill. He did the same for my brothers and sisters and basically to everyone around him. He believed that every single human had a unique purpose to fulfill and that each of us was of infinite worth and potential, not to be compared to anyone else.

He was a great teacher, first by his example, and then by his words, and I was deeply influenced by his insights. One of the fundamental things he continually taught me is that there are two ways to live: a life of primary greatness or a life of secondary greatness. Primary greatness is who you really are—your character, your integrity, your deepest motives and desires. Secondary greatness is popularity, title, position, fame, fortune, and honors. He taught me not to worry about secondary greatness and to focus on primary greatness. He also noted that secondary greatness would often—but not always—follow those who achieve primary greatness, and that primary greatness had its own intrinsic rewards, such as peace of mind, contribution, and rich and rewarding relationships. These rewards far outweigh the extrinsic rewards of secondary greatness—money, popularity, and the self-absorbed, pleasure-ridden life that we too often consider "success."

This book is a collection of several of my father's best essays that have never appeared in book form before and aren't well known. But they are vintage Stephen Covey and contain some of his best thinking. So, my colleagues and I thought it only appropriate to share them with the world. At the writing of this foreword, it has been three years since my father died. But in these essays you will hear his insightful and penetrating voice speaking to your core. These essays are virtually untouched from when he first wrote them. We have simply woven them into a narrative about living a life of primary greatness. My father wrote some of these while he was formulating

The 7 Habits of Highly Effective People, and it's exciting to see in these articles the genesis of ideas that have since transformed the world of business and many millions of lives. But this is not *The 7 Habits* all over again. This book contains refreshing insights about moving from a life absorbed with the external trappings of success to a life of deep peace, satisfaction, and wisdom.

Many people are hurting. They have chronic life problems, dissatisfactions, and disappointments. There's a lot of discouragement, and much of what is passed off as a "cure" for these ailments is just superficial. This book can give you real healing in a world of aspirin and bandages. I've faced some wrenching tests in my own life, and I can tell you from personal experience that the principles I learned from my father—principles clearly taught in this book—have given my family and me the courage and the confidence to move forward, make a contribution, and find happiness. Those principles will do the same for you.

PREFACE
PRIMARY VS. SECONDARY GREATNESS

There were 614 wooden deck chairs on the *Titanic* when it put to sea for its first and last voyage. Every morning the crew would untie the chairs and arrange them attractively so the passengers could lounge on the deck. Passengers could arrange them any way they liked.[1]

Presumably, no one was actually rearranging the deck chairs as the great *Titanic* sank.

But "rearranging deck chairs on the *Titanic*" is now shorthand for doing pointless or trivial things instead of the important things in life.

Rearranging deck chairs while the ship is sinking is literally the last thing you'd do.

Then why is it the first thing so many of us do?

To rearrange deck chairs is to put appearances before reality, to care more about image than substance, to have your priorities backward.

And that's what we do. We put last things first.

The result? Missed goals, failed careers, broken families, bad health, faltering companies, lost friendships, a life swallowed up in the debris of poor decisions.

That's what happened to the *Titanic*, which sank in 1912 with 1,517 dead. "Safety first" was put last. The ship had been plowing at high speed through dangerous ice fields. There weren't enough lifeboats for all the passengers. There were no lifeboat drills, so they didn't know what to do when disaster struck.[2]

The story of the *Titanic* reminds us of the truth of Goethe's saying, "Things that matter most must never be at the mercy of things that matter least."

How many of us tend to put last things first?

Do we put our hidden agendas ahead of the people we're responsible for?

Are we nice to people's faces but then bad-mouth them behind their backs?

Do we treat strangers better than we treat our own family members—the people who matter most to us?

Do we take as much as we can in return for giving as little as we can?

Do we put long-term success at the mercy of short-term success?

Do we value the trappings of success (deck chairs) more than the inner peace and satisfaction that come from making a real contribution (saving the ship)?

According to Dr. Stephen R. Covey, *primary greatness* is the kind of success that comes from contribution. By contrast, the trappings of success—position, popularity, public image—are *secondary greatness*. When you see the actions and behaviors of celebrities, famous athletes, CEOs, movie actors, or whatever, you're seeing secondary greatness.

Primary greatness is on the inside. It's about character. Secondary greatness is on the outside. As Dr. Covey taught, "Many people with secondary greatness—that is, social recognition for their talents—lack primary greatness or goodness in their character. Sooner or later, you'll see this in every long-term relationship they have, whether it is with a business associate, a spouse, a friend, or a teenage child going through an identity crisis. It is character that communicates most eloquently. As Emerson once put it, 'What you are shouts so loudly in my ears that I cannot hear what you say.'"[3]

A successful life is about primary greatness—a life of duty, honor, integrity, perseverance, self-sacrifice, and service, regardless of material rewards or circumstances. These are natural, universal, unbreakable principles. They are the same for everyone everywhere and for all time. Going for secondary greatness without primary greatness doesn't work. People don't build successful lives on the unstable sands of what is outwardly or temporarily popular, but they do build successful lives on the bedrock of principles that do not change.

Ironically, secondary greatness often—but not always—follows primary greatness. People of good character tend to win at life because people trust them. Their hard work usually brings a certain level of security and, sometimes, even prosperity. Their service ethic earns them the love and loyalty of others. These are natural consequences of primary greatness.

Of course, there are no guarantees: People of good character can get sick or have bad luck, just like anyone else. There are plenty of decent people who work hard all their lives without prospering financially. But people who seek primary greatness enjoy a kind of peace and satisfaction that cannot come to those who strive for secondary greatness but know there's nothing substantial inside.

Many people confuse success with secondary greatness. That means they do everything they can to seem successful on the outside, while hiding from who they really are on the inside. They won't pay the price to be truly successful. They look for ways to succeed without putting in the effort. They project a false image. They pretend to be your friend. Most of us have been guilty of this kind of thinking at one time or another.

It should be obvious that negative traits like egotism, idleness, procrastination, and dishonesty have natural consequences, just as positive virtues do. However, in the age of secondary greatness, polls seem to matter more than moral convictions, and what's on the outside has become more consequential than what is on the inside.

Still, deep down in the innermost part of the self, we know that we can't live successful lives that are not also lives of principle. "Gallup Polls show that over 90 percent of American adults support the teaching of honesty, democracy, acceptance of people of different races and ethnic backgrounds, patriotism, caring for friends and family members, moral courage, and the Golden Rule."[4] At our core, we know that outward success is failure if it isn't rooted in inner success. We want that for our children. We should also want it for ourselves.

This intuition is backed up by good data. Scientists interested in finding out which skills and traits lead to success no longer focus so much on intelligence or talent; many now see character as a more significant determiner of success. For example, the famous Perry Preschool Project has tracked people over decades to isolate the factors that lead to fulfilling lives and true accomplishment. Begun in Michigan in 1965, the project involved 123 preschool children whose lives have been studied ever since. As children, the Perry treatment-group members were drawn from deep inner-city poverty and taught to "persist at a boring and often unrewarding task . . . to delay gratification . . . to follow through on a plan." In other words, basic character strengths. A half century later, those teachings are still paying off in the lives of the Perry group members. Compared to their contemporaries, they have been significantly more likely to graduate, twice as likely to be employed and earn a good wage, and half as likely to be arrested or spend time on welfare.[5]

Ironically, the Perry Project was intended to raise the IQ of the students. That didn't happen, but it's easy to see that their SQ, or "success quotient," rose wonderfully as they internalized the principles of a good character.

Dr. Covey felt strongly that inner character was far more significant a factor in success than talent or intelligence or circumstances. He spent his life helping people around the world recognize that fundamental truth and transform their lives. Thousands have done so through corporate and government training or just through reading his best-selling books. Today in schools and colleges on every continent those principles are taught to young people through *The Leader in Me*, a whole-school process and system offered by FranklinCovey. The results are nothing short of remarkable, as students learn the difference between primary and secondary greatness, and how to live lives of primary greatness.

How do we internalize the principles of primary greatness? Isn't character fixed at birth? Is it even possible to change our character?

Although it's not easy, character change is possible. As Dr. Covey taught, we *can* change because we have the power to choose how we will act. Human character might be like a recipe—a cup of genetics, a tablespoon of environment, and a few ounces of luck—but we get to decide what we will make out of all those ingredients.

The key to success is to align ourselves to unchangeable principles and stop taking detours away from them. If you want to go directly north, you align your nose to the needle on the compass. Any deviation, and you're no longer headed toward true north; that's just reality. The principles that govern reality are the same principles that govern success, and if you violate those principles, you will suffer the consequences.

You won't necessarily feel guilty or even uncomfortable if you violate a principle, at least not immediately. You might even feel what researchers call the "cheater's high"—the satisfying feeling of getting away with it. Many people get pleasure out of cheating on their taxes, padding their expense accounts, or bad-mouthing somebody. They may congratulate themselves and feel superior to the poor saps who don't cheat.[6]

However, most of us know deep down when we are hurting others—or ourselves—and the consequences to our character are inescapable.

If you violate the principle of saving by spending too much, you'll tend to be poor. If you make a habit of violating the principles that govern your physical body, like exercise and proper nutrition, you'll probably end up weak and sick. If you violate the principles of kindness and respect, you'll almost certainly end up with more enemies than friends.

Of course, none of these consequences of bad behavior are absolutely inevitable. But if you look at life through the cold, realistic lens of probability, they are more than likely to happen.

The principles that govern reality are inarguable. They are beyond our control. They don't care if we believe in them—they simply *are*. Thus, we're more likely to succeed in life if we align ourselves to those principles and stop trying to ignore them.

That means examining our character and motives. If we want success in life, we might have to realign our character and motives to different principles. We might have to work on a character flaw, such as procrastination or envy or selfishness. In any case, we have to confront who we really are inside and align our lives to principles that govern success.

It can be difficult to enter what Dr. Covey calls the "secret garden" of our lives and find out what's actually growing there. It's not easy to realign to true principles, but it's the only way to real success.

Principles are like levers. It might be impossible to move a boulder by yourself; but if you use a lever, it can be relatively easy. And the longer and stronger the lever, the easier it gets. As Archimedes said, "Give me a lever long enough . . . and I can move the world!" Principles like integrity, service, and priority have great leverage. Only by consistently applying these levers can you hope to dislodge the biggest obstacles to your success—lapses of character such as selfishness, victimism, and "fatal distractions" from true priorities. If you're a person of integrity, people will easily trust you. You'll get much further with most people by giving them good service than by treating them with indifference. By putting your true priorities first, you won't have to pay the heavy price of wasting your time and your life.

In this book, Dr. Covey describes how to make that important journey from an obsession with secondary greatness to a focus on primary greatness. He then describes twelve of the highest-leverage

principles successful people live by, giving guidance as to how to internalize those principles:

> Integrity
> Contribution
> Priority
> Personal Sacrifice
> Service
> Responsibility
> Loyalty
> Reciprocity
> Diversity
> Continuous Learning
> Renewal
> Teaching to Learn

The first lever is integrity, the state of being whole and undivided. People with integrity are the same on the inside and the outside. They have no hidden agendas, no ulterior motives. They are, as Dr. Covey says, "totally integrated around a set of correct principles."

We will be truly successful only if our goal is total integrity at our innermost core. Once we have set that goal for ourselves, primary greatness is within our grasp. The twelve levers take us from seeming successful to being successful; from deep-down insecurity to the inner confidence people feel when they anchor their lives in natural principles.

Why these twelve levers?

Clear back to ancient times, thoughtful people have made many such lists of useful principles. Aristotle's table of virtues and Benjamin Franklin's thirteen virtues come to mind. And in our time, the eminent psychologist Dr. Martin Seligman's twenty-four character strengths are based on serious research into what makes the good life possible.[7]

Dr. Covey's twelve levers are based on his own deep research and long experience working with thousands of people around the globe. For him, they were fundamental and inescapable, and there is something of a hierarchy about them. As noted, *integrity* is the foundation of real success, along with *contribution*—the principle of leaving a meaningful legacy, of making a positive difference. Living by the principle of *priority* enables us to make that contribution without losing our way in the thick of thin things.

It's impossible to achieve any lasting legacy without *personal sacrifice*. When we begin to ask what we can do to be of *service* to others, we begin to understand what it means to get beyond the ego and taste true success.

The natural principle of *responsibility* is neglected more and more in our world. Nobody has any trouble taking responsibility for success, but the distinction between people of primary and secondary greatness becomes very clear when it's time to account for things that don't work out so well. Then the person of primary greatness blames no one else but steps forward and frankly accepts responsibility when it's due.

Loyalty is the natural consequence of serving others. As you persevere in dedicated service, you build up tremendous equity in your relationships. You grow in loyalty to them and they grow in loyalty to you. Closely related to loyalty is the law of *reciprocity*—it is just as constant as the law of gravity. We all have consequences of our daily actions paid over to us at the end of every minute of our lives, and the balance can be in our favor or against us. We will be treated as we treat others. To violate a trust invites a reciprocal violation. It might not come immediately, but the price will be paid in time.

At the core of our being, we must value *diversity* if we want to maximize our success in life. Whether you're talking about biology or business, politics or product development, nature kills off sameness and celebrates differences. As Dr. Covey says, "If two people have the same opinion, one of them is unnecessary." As we learn to

value and leverage the diverse strengths different people bring, we are far likelier to succeed.

Finally, without *continuous learning* and *self-renewal*, we face the natural consequences of stagnation and irrelevance. We renew ourselves through exercise, reading, making time for loved ones, and rejuvenating practices like meditation. We internalize the principles of primary greatness by *teaching to learn*—that is, becoming not just an exemplar but a teacher of primary greatness.

Taken together, the twelve levers make your life easier and more fruitful. By using these levers, you strengthen your character and your influence with other people. You'll still work hard to move the boulders of life, but your efforts will no longer be futile.

These twelve levers are not the sum total of the principles of success—there are many others—but they are the indispensable principles. Without them, no one can truly succeed. This book looks deeply into these principles and helps us understand how to make them part of our inner selves.

Primary greatness is the natural consequence of pushing on these levers.

An act of kindness has great power.

An understanding friend has tremendous influence.

A responsible worker gains more and more responsibility.

A person with integrity has a lot of moral muscle.

As Dr. Covey taught, "If you want to have a happy marriage, be the kind of person who generates positive energy and sidesteps negative energy rather than empowering it. If you want to have a more pleasant, cooperative teenager, be a more understanding, empathic, consistent, loving parent. If you want to have more freedom, more latitude in your job, be a more responsible, a more helpful, a more contributing employee. If you want to be trusted, be trustworthy. If you want the secondary greatness of recognized talent, focus first on primary greatness of character."[8]

The influence of Dr. Stephen R. Covey is nothing short of a global phenomenon. Starting with the 1989 publication of *The 7 Habits of Highly Effective People*, millions of leaders, educators, and families worldwide have drawn inspiration and comfort from Dr. Covey's affirming, inspiring voice. If that voice is familiar to you, it's because his language has become the language of our time—affirming phrases such as "be proactive" and "think win-win" and "seek first to understand" have reshaped the culture we live in.

But Dr. Covey had much more than *The 7 Habits* to contribute. The editors of this new book went through dozens of articles published by Dr. Covey to isolate more of his insights into the principles of successful living. The powerful readings in this book have been inaccessible until now. If you are like millions of others, Dr. Covey's meditations on the levers of primary greatness can transform your life from good to great.

—Stephen Covey's colleagues

I

HOW TO ACHIEVE PRIMARY GREATNESS

CHAPTER 1

THE SECRET LIFE

If you look the right way, you can see that the whole world is a garden.

—FRANCES HODGSON BURNETT

We all live three lives: public, private, and secret. The secret life is where your heart is, where your real motives are—the ultimate desires of your life. It is also the source of primary greatness. If you have the courage to explore your secret life, you can honestly question your deepest motivations. Are you prepared to rescript those motivations— to realign your life to the core principles of true success?

The secret life is the key to primary greatness.

In New York City, I attended the Broadway play *The Secret Garden*. The play was particularly poignant for me, because my mother had just died.

The Tony Award—winning musical is the story of a young girl whose mother and father die of cholera in India as the play begins. She is sent to live with her uncle in a large British manor. The old house is filled with romantic spirits. As the restless girl explores the grounds of the estate, she discovers the entrance to the magical secret garden, a place where anything is possible.

When she first enters the garden, she finds that it appears to be dead, much like her cousin, a bedridden boy, and her uncle, still haunted by memories of his lovely wife who died giving birth to the boy. In harmony with natural laws and principles, the girl faithfully plants seeds and brings new life to the garden. As the roots are warmed and the garden cultivated, she brings about a dramatic transformation of her entire family culture within one season.

In my many years of teaching and training, I have seen several such transformations brought about by proactive people who live by principles of greatness in their secret, private, and public lives.

When I returned home the next day to speak at my mother's funeral, I referred to *The Secret Garden*, because for me and many others, my mother's home was a secret garden where we could escape and be nurtured by positive affirmation. In her eyes, all about us was good, and all that was good was possible.

Our Three Lives

In our public life, we are seen and heard by colleagues, associates, and others within our circle. In our private life, we interact more intimately with spouses, family members, and close friends. The secret life is part of the other two.

The secret life is the mainspring that motivates the other two lives. Many people never visit the secret life. Their public and private lives are essentially scripted by whom and what precedes and surrounds them or by the pressures of the environment. Thus, they never exercise that unique endowment of self-awareness—the key to the secret life—where you can stand apart from yourself and observe yourself.

Courage is required to explore your secret life because you must first withdraw from the social mirror—the reflection of ourselves that society feeds back to us but may have little to do with our inner selves. We get used to the view of ourselves in the social mirror. And we may opt to avoid self-examination and idle away our time in a vacuum of reverie and rationalization. In that frame of mind, we have little sense of identity, safety, or security.

> *The secret life is where your heart is, where your real motives are— the ultimate desires of your life.*

Examine Your Motives

The most critical junctures in my life take place when I visit my secret life and ask, "What do I think? What do I believe is right? What should my motives be?" These are times when I deeply visit my secret life and choose my motives. "Wait a minute," I say to myself. "It's my life. I can choose how to use my time and energy. I can choose whether to get up in the morning and exercise. I can choose to get angry or not. I can choose whether I want to make reconciliation with this person or not. I can choose my own motives."

One of the exciting fruits of the secret life is the ability to consciously choose your own motives. Until you choose your own motives, you really can't choose to live your own life. Everything flows out of motives and motivation—they are the root of our deepest desires. The question is, which motives will we put first in our lives?

When I face a frustrating or perplexing situation, I enter into my secret life. That's where I face myself and ask, "Will I live by correct principles, or will I surrender to the demands of secondary greatness?"

As I learn to be proactive in exploring the secret life, I tap into self-awareness, imagination, conscience, and into the exercise of free will to choose my motives.

For example, when thinking about your career, you might ask, "Now, what is my real motive?" N. Eldon Tanner, former Speaker of the Alberta Legislative Assembly and former Cabinet member, once said, "Whenever I had a big career decision, I had to visit my heart and ask, 'Am I totally prepared to put first things first—and in this position, will I keep my priorities straight?'" He said, "I'd have to struggle with that question until it was settled." Once he had made that decision, he would look at the assignment and ask, "If it would build the causes most dear to me, I will go and serve there." He became well respected throughout his country.

> *Until you choose your own motives, you really can't choose to live your own life. Everything flows out of motives and motivation—they are the root of our deepest desires.*

I met with this great man once when I was serving on a search committee for a new university president. When I entered his office, he left his desk and came around, sat next to me, and said, "What do you want me to understand?" He listened to me with much intensity and sincerity, then said, "I want you to know how much I respect you." It deeply impressed me.

People who regularly explore their secret life and examine their motives are better able to see into the heart of others, practice empathy, empower them, and affirm their worth and identity.

A healthy secret life will benefit your private and public lives in many ways. For example, when I'm preparing to give a speech, I read aloud a favorite discourse that is inspiring to me because it helps me clarify my motive. I lose all desire to impress. My only desire is to serve. And when I go to a public setting with that motive, I have great confidence and inner peace. I feel more love for the people and feel much more authentic myself.

Executives I have consulted with tell me, "This is the first time in many, many years that I've done any soul searching. I've seen myself as if for the first time, and I've resolved that my life is going to be different. I'm going to try to be true to what I really believe." Over the years, many people have written me to say, "Your principles have made the difference. I'd never really thought about some of them before, but I resonate with them." That's because these principles reside in their secret lives.

And yet, most of us spend our busy days privately doing our thing, never pausing long enough to enter the secret life, the secret garden, where we can create masterpieces, discover great truths, and enhance every aspect of our public and private lives.

A healthy secret life is the key to primary greatness.

Self-Affirmation

A key to having a healthy secret life is self-affirmation. Among the most important bits of communication are messages of affirmation you give yourself and others.

A good self-affirmation has five characteristics:

> It's personal, meaning it is written in the first person.
> It's positive rather than negative, meaning that it affirms what is good and right.
> It's present tense, meaning you are doing it now or have the potential for doing it.
> It's visual, meaning you can see it clearly in your mind's eye.
> It's emotional, meaning you have strong feelings attached to it.

The following two examples of affirmation will serve to illustrate these five principles.

OVERREACTION. Suppose a parent who overreacts to spilled milk decides he has the potential for improvement. Thus, he resolves to respond with wisdom, love, firmness, fairness, patience, and self-control in stressful situations. He then writes his resolve in the form of an affirmation:

"How deeply satisfying (emotional) it is to me (personal) to respond (present tense) under conditions of fatigue, stress, pressure, or disappointment (visual conditions) with self-control, wisdom, firmness, patience, and love (positive)."

PROCRASTINATION. Suppose an individual desires to improve in the area of procrastination. Because she compulsively puts things off and manages by crisis, she selects as her desired behavior to be on top of things, to be current and value-driven. Her affirmation becomes: "How satisfying and exhilarating it is to be in charge of myself, guiding my own destiny, by taking time to plan, to work my plan, and to delegate to others."

Power of Self-Affirmation

Norman Cousins, author of *Anatomy of an Illness* and *Human Options*, showed the world how the power of affirmation enables us to release within us our frequently untapped emotional strengths.

Within a week of returning home from a trip abroad, Cousins found himself almost unable to move his neck, arms, hands, fingers, and legs. Soon hospitalized, he was diagnosed as suffering from a serious disease of the connective tissues. His doctor told him, "Your chance for full recovery is one in five hundred."

At first, Cousins allowed his doctor and the hospital to do their thing. Medication was administered—often in excess. Tests were performed—both routinely and redundantly. All these medical procedures, plus his doctor's unfavorable diagnosis, gave Cousins a great deal to think about. "It seemed clear to me," he later wrote, "that if I were to be that one in five hundred, I had better be something more than a passive observer."

Familiar with research detailing the negative effects of negative emotions on body chemistry, he asked: "Wouldn't positive emotions produce positive effects? Is it possible that love, hope, faith, laughter, confidence, and the will to live have therapeutic value?"

Reasoning that if the negative is true, then the positive must also be true, Cousins soon formulated a plan for the pursuit of affirmative emotions. His plan drew upon medical resources, supportive professionals, laughter, and the love of his family. He then walked out of the hospital, secured a room in a hotel, hired his own nurse, and watched Marx Brothers movies and television comedies. Ten minutes of a deep belly laugh, he found, provided him with two or three hours of pain-free sleep—the first in months. He discovered that the mind is a walking apothecary, a carry-it-with-you drugstore.

Week by week, Norman Cousins gained strength. Year by year, his mobility improved. And in spite of speculation by some that his efforts had nothing to do with his recovery, that he would have recovered had he done nothing or that he was simply the beneficiary of an experiment in self-administered placebos, Cousins believed that his experience was, and is, proof of the power of the will to live and the power of imagination to release and unleash enormous powers innate in us.

Three Helpful Practices

I have found the following three practices to be very helpful in the process of self-affirmation.

1. USE RELAXATION TECHNIQUES TO PLANT AFFIRMATIONS. Affirmations can't achieve effective results in the rush of everyday living. The mind and the body must slow down. By learning to relax, we can learn to slow down. When we are in a deeply relaxed state, our brain waves become very slow; they are then highly suggestible. Through visual and emotional affirmations, we can plant ideas and images deep within us. The challenge, of course, is to learn to relax.

There are many techniques for relaxing. One of the best is to consciously tense your muscle groups and then relax them. The theory behind this technique is that if you can tense a muscle, then logically you should be able to relax it. Another technique is to mentally relax so that you see yourself as limp as a rag doll. Or you visualize all of your muscles becoming limp and long. You see yourself in your mind's eye becoming heavy from your feet up through your legs, your torso, and your arms, to your neck, your back, and your face.

During the twilight periods—upon arising and just before retiring—the brain waves are much slower. This becomes a prime programming opportunity, because the subconscious mind is more receptive than at any other time of day. I have used the principle of relaxation as it applies to affirmations with my own children and have seen dramatic results.

2. USE REPETITION TO ENSURE SUCCESS. If you desire to use your affirmation to initiate change or to prepare yourself for some future event, you must experience it over and over again. Say it, see it, feel it. Make it a part of you. Remember, you are programming yourself. You are eclipsing and subordinating the earlier scripts written into your makeup. Instead of living the scripts given by your parents, your friends, society, the environment, or genetics, you're affirming; you're living the new scripts you've chosen for yourself. By repeating affirmations, you can grow and change.

3. USE IMAGINATION AND VISUALIZATION TO SEE THE CHANGE. In any affirmation, the more details you can see in your mind's eye, and the more clear and vivid the details—the color of your office drapes, the texture of the floor on your bare feet as you serve breakfast, the opened planning book on your desk, your daughter's report card—the less you will view your affirmation as a spectator and the more you will experience it as a participant. The more senses you can employ in visualizing a change, the greater chance of actually rescripting your life. Most of us neglect this creative power.

We live too much out of our memories, too little out of our imagination—too much on what is or has been, not enough on what can be. That's like trying to drive forward by looking in the rearview mirror.

> *We live too much out of our memories, too little out of our imagination—too much on what is or has been, not enough on what can be. That's like trying to drive forward by looking in the rearview mirror.*

In manned space programs, part of the astronauts' training includes many hours in spaceflight simulators, training or programming their minds and bodies to accomplish tasks in situations no human has experienced. When the astronauts were ultimately faced with these new challenges in space, they performed unbelievably well because of their simulated experiences. Imagination and creativity had provided the mental images for events that would take place in the future. Their minds, unencumbered by conventional censors, were free to become flexible, adaptive, uninhibited—truly creative and innovative.

Use the power of self-affirmation daily, in your secret garden, to cultivate your own meaningful life.

Application & Suggestions

> Consider keeping a personal journal in order to track your
> progress toward primary greatness. Many of the application
> suggestions in this book encourage you to record thoughts
> and create written plans.
> Write in your personal journal the answers to these ques-
> tions:
>> In what ways have you been chasing secondary great-
>> ness at the expense of primary greatness?
>> Ask yourself: "What do I believe is right? What are my
>> deepest moral convictions? What should I do with my
>> life?" Write down what you discover about yourself.
> One of the exciting fruits of the "secret garden" is the abil-
> ity to consciously choose your own motives. What motives
> do you need to change? Record your best motives and what
> you can do to actualize them.
> Consider the steps to create a good self-affirmation state-
> ment. Write the script you usually tell yourself. Now *rewrite*
> that script. What can you affirm about yourself? What's
> good or even great about you and about the contribution
> you can make?

CHAPTER 2

CHARACTER: THE SOURCE OF PRIMARY GREATNESS

Our character is what we do when we think no one is looking.

—H. JACKSON BROWNE

Character, what you are, is ultimately more important than competence, what you can do. Primary greatness is, at its base, a matter of character.

I emphasize the preeminence of character in the lives of people because I believe character (what a person is) is ultimately more important than competence (what a person can do). Obviously, both are important, but character is foundational. All else builds on this cornerstone.

> *Character, what you are, is ultimately more important than competence, what you can do.*

Even the very best structure, system, style, and skills can't compensate completely for deficiencies in character.

Also, I believe courage and consideration are the key building blocks of emotional maturity, and that emotional maturity is foundational to all decisions and all relationships.

The emotionally mature person is also highly effective. Mature people may have a healthy ego, but they also have high respect for other people. They balance the courage of their commitment to principles with consideration for others.

Maturity—A Balance Between Courage and Consideration

I first learned that maturity is a balance between courage and consideration from one of my professors at the Harvard Business School, Hrand Saxenian. At the time, Hrand was working on his own doctoral thesis on the subject.

This is how he taught it: Emotional maturity is the ability to express your feelings and convictions with courage, balanced with consideration for the feelings and convictions of others.

The truth of that idea struck me powerfully. But even more powerful was the way he modeled it. For instance, when we entered the statistics portion of the course, he told the class that he didn't know much about statistics, and that he would be learning along with us. He also acknowledged what our feelings might be, as we were in competition with other students and sections and had to take a schoolwide exam.

In self-defense, we sent a delegation to the dean's office to ask for a new statistics teacher. We told the dean that we liked Mr. Saxenian as a teacher, but that his ignorance of statistics would put us at a disadvantage when we took the tests. To our annoyance, the dean simply said, "Well, just do the best you can." So we went back to Hrand, and with his help, we got some technical notes and passed them around. In a sense, we taught each other statistics. And our section, out of eight, finished second in the exams.

I'm convinced we did well on the exams because Hrand had the courage to confess his ignorance of the subject and the consideration to help us come up with a solution. Hrand showed us that courage balanced with consideration was common to great leaders. In fact, he went back through history to show how the truly great leaders who built strong cultures behind a shared vision were those who had these two characteristics of emotional maturity, who beautifully balanced courage and consideration.

In a different way, I have also tested this idea. First, I have gone back into the history of management thought, interpersonal relationships theory, and human psychology theory, and I have found the same two concepts. For instance, the transactional-analysis theory Thomas Harris made popular in his book *I'm Okay, You're Okay* really had its theoretical roots in both Eric Berne's *Games People Play* and Sigmund Freud and his psychoanalytic theories. Well, what is "I'm okay, you're okay" but courage balanced with consideration? "I'm okay, you're not okay" means I have courage, but little respect or consideration for you. "I'm not okay, you're okay" suggests no ego strength, no courage. And "I'm not okay, you're not okay" suggests little courage and not much consideration.

Then I looked at the research of Robert Blake and Jane Mouton, the great theorists who looked at success from two dimensions: "Are you task-oriented or are you people-oriented?" Some are low in one area, some in both. The ideal, of course, is high people orientation plus high task orientation. In other words, high courage to drive the task to completion, plus high respect and consideration for others.

The concept of win-win is essentially the same thing: You have high respect for self to ensure that you win, but you work in a way that enables other people to win as well. If you're synergistic, combining your strengths with theirs, you create far better solutions, as manifest in mission statements, decisions, strategic partnerships, and customer and employee relations. The win-lose approach is symptomatic of high respect for self, and low regard for others and their situation. The lose-win approach suggests low respect for self, and high regard for other people.

I examined other psychological theories and found that they all focus on the same two factors. Sometimes *courage* is called *respect, confidence, tough-mindedness*, or *ego strength*; and *consideration* may be called *empathy* or *kindheartedness*. I also found that same balance in the great philosophical and religious literature: "Treat others as you want to be treated" is an expression of this synergistic spirit.

Finally, I've interviewed many winners of the Malcolm Baldrige Award, which is given periodically to people and organizations that show dramatic improvements in the quality of their products or services. I have asked them the question, "What is the most difficult challenge you faced?" And they always say, "Giving up control." In effect, they are saying, "We had to create synergistic relationships with all stakeholders. We had to reach the point where we really believed in other people, in a bone-deep way, not in some personality-ethic manner. We also had to learn to be strong in expressing how we see things."

Essentially, the Baldrige winners learned to Think Win-Win; Seek First to Understand, Then to Be Understood; and Synergize (which are Habits 4, 5, and 6 of my 7 Habits). By practicing these habits, they gained new insights and skills, opened new options, engaged in more partnering and bonding, and boosted creativity. But it has to come out of this deep spirit of win-win, of courage balanced with consideration.

Improved Results and Relationships

Balancing courage with consideration is a good way to achieve improved results and better relationships. Without this balance, you tend to get one at the expense of the other. For instance, I once worked with the president of a large organization who was a task-oriented person. If he needed to build relationships to get results, he could charm the socks off anybody, but it was always with regard to a task. The task defined the relationship. In other words, once he built the relationship, he would then get on with the task. I have known other people who were the opposite. They are so needful of relationships that they work relationships through tasks.

In searching for the factors that govern success in business, David McClelland, one of the great research psychologists at Harvard, developed what he called his need-achievement inventory. He would give people different pictures, and then have them make up a story based on the pictures. After listening to their stories, McClelland would profile the candidate, then give his recommendations to employers to match the profile of the person with the requirements of the job. He tended to classify people according to their need for power, affiliation, or achievement. In a sense, McClelland was looking at this concept of inward motivation. He identified character as the critical factor of long-term success.

Character Over Competency

Even though people may be technically well educated, if they don't grow in emotional maturity, eventually their skills may be their undoing. For instance, the task-oriented president I mentioned earlier exhausted his social capital with his board of directors to the point at which he no longer had power or influence with them. The board would not sustain the president and they had to make a change. Board members felt that they were being manipulated by one superlative presentation after another, one big charmer after another. Eventually, the chickens came home to roost. Skills don't trump character, yet the training and education of most people is designed to build competence, not character.

So how can we meet the equally important need for ongoing character development?

Find out how the people around you, those who have a stake

in your success, measure your character. You could do this through a 360-degree stakeholder information system, which gives people solid, scientific, systematic feedback on their performance in both dimensions. A 360-degree survey gets information about a person from all stakeholders: employees, customers, supervisors, and co-workers. Then the person will say, "Gosh, I have low marks for team building and interdependency, even though I'm producing the numbers. What can I do?" Now they recognize where they need to work on character development. They can then organize resources to draw on: their families, their friends, professional association, church, and support groups.

Humility and Courage: The Source of Virtues

I maintain that humility is the mother of virtues, because humility helps us center our lives on principles. Humility helps us see the need for ongoing character development. Humility helps us be considerate of others. I would then say that courage is the father of all virtues. Together courage and consideration help us become fully integrated as individuals. Karl Jung said that we never achieve individuation—the total integration of the human personality—until our later years. People must go through different phases of individuation. It takes a great deal of experience, going around the block many times in many ways, before we gradually come to see the consequences of erring on one side or the other, and gradually achieve an integration of our internal character.

That's why you need to be patient with yourself to build strong character. People who start small and push a little every day at these high-leverage principles will expand their influence until they truly become models of good character and, eventually, mentors and teachers of other people. They become change catalysts and Transi-

PRIMARY GREATNESS \ 19

tion Persons who can break cycles of negative behavior in their families, organizations, or communities.

For example, I once had an experience with the top partners of an international firm. They were grappling with the fact that many of their people had lots of competency but little consideration. In other words, they were smart but rude. "It shows in the way we admit people, the way we make them partners, the way we reward them. We have a low-trust culture. No wonder we're losing some of our best minds. We have a political atmosphere where everyone is reading the tea leaves. We have moved so far away from our founding principles."

In the last analysis, it's the character in the culture that counts; yet, we let many character-destroying forces have their way with us until we lose the original character of the founders of the company or until we become programs ourselves, not programmers. And so we must begin the process of reprogramming to push on the levers of primary greatness.

Writing New Programs

How can we reprogram ourselves? Well, often we must first be humbled, either by circumstances, such as not getting desired results and losing our assets, or by crises, not getting the meaning or fulfillment we desire, or failing to maintain good relationships with our colleagues, spouses, and kids. We are then more willing to accept the fact that universal principles like respect, empathy, honesty, and trust ultimately govern. We are then more willing to accept responsibility for who and what we are. We are then more willing to develop and live by a solid sense of mission, which does much to produce integrity. Ultimately, *what we are* (character) is the most critical component of success.

In fact, I've concluded that the only way I can grow toward the ideal balance between competency and character is by living true to my conscience, to the principles that I know are right. If I begin in any way to falter in either competency or character, I can usually trace my failures within a few hours, if not days, to some flaw in the integrity of my life.

We read of actors who feel that they were exploited in certain roles and parts early in their careers. But as they gain more respect, they turn down scripts and roles that aren't supportive of their new vision of themselves. They may even write their own scripts or determine what parts they play. We can also do the same in our careers.

I'm convinced that we can write and live our own scripts—more than most people acknowledge. I also know the price that must be paid. It's a struggle. It requires visualization and affirmation. It involves living a life of integrity, starting with making and keeping promises, until the whole human personality—the senses, the thinking, the feeling, and the intuition—are no longer in conflict.

Character Development and Personal Discipline

Many people need to break with the physical and emotional addictions that hold them down and reduce their quality of life. Until that happens, there can be little progress because the body is controlling the will. Once the break is made, people then have a path to progress. If they can get some degree of control over their appetites, they can have some degree of control over their passions, and even begin to structure their motivations and desires. Their character development can then skyrocket. It's like breaking away from the tremendous gravitational pull of the earth and breaking out into space where there is flexibility and freedom.

We all struggle with these physical habits and appetites daily. Personally, I know that I have to keep myself under the influence of wisdom, conscience, and correct principles, or else sooner or later I suffer the effects directly, or those around me start to suffer. Violating one principle can lead to violating another; for example, I find that if I gorge at dinner, I might not be sensitive later to other people's feelings. I have to live in control. Anytime I start feeling angry, if I go into self-analysis, I can usually trace that anger back to some indiscretion or indulgence on my part. I may justify and rationalize my behavior, but if I go counter to my conscience, I know it weakens my will. And I know it affects the level of consideration I have for the needs and feelings of others.

With the strong foundation of character in place, we can add all the colorful elements of personality. If you don't have the character roots, you might pretend to play the part, but when push comes to shove, you'll be uprooted. Such uprooting is among our most difficult learning experiences, but also among the most powerful and useful ones as we recommit to live lives of integrity.

Application & Suggestions

> Develop a Personal Mission Statement based on a vision of your life—a vision of contribution to your family, your organization, your community. Write a statement that is based on principles that will not change.
> In your communications with others, consider your personal balance between courage and consideration. Are you able to express your feelings and convictions with courage while balancing them with consideration for the feelings and convictions of others? The next time you're in a high-stakes conversation, deliberately try to strike that balance.
> How are you balancing your own productivity with your production capability? For one day, track how much time you spend being productive. Then compare it to the amount of time you spend increasing your production

capability—that is, exercising, reading, learning, building relationships with others. In your personal journal, write your reflections on this exercise. What did you learn? What do you need to change?

> Physical and emotional addictions constrict our mind and spirit. Most of us have ingrained habits that hold us back. What holds you back? What steps could you take to break free? Make a goal to break one poor habit or to develop one habit that will strengthen you and improve your life.

CHAPTER 3

HOW TO ALIGN YOURSELF TO PRINCIPLES

Change your opinions, keep to your principles;
Change your leaves, keep intact your roots.

—VICTOR HUGO

Principles and natural laws are absolute, inarguable, and always relevant. This truth is the foundation of successful living. Primary greatness is, above all, living a life centered on principles. In this chapter, we'll find out how to get to that center.

The key to primary greatness is to be centered on principles. We're not in control of our world; principles are in control. We're arrogant when we think we are in control. Yes, we may control our actions, but not the consequences of our actions. Those are controlled by principles—by natural laws.

Building character and quality of life is a function of aligning our beliefs and behaviors with universal principles. These principles are impersonal, external, factual, objective, and self-evident. They operate regardless of our awareness of them or our obedience or disobedience to them.

Why Center on Principles?

Now, some people have asked me why I make a big deal out of the difference between principles and values. They say, "I have my values. They're as good as anyone's." To me, the distinction is vital because most people think values are principles. In fact, one CEO told me, "Our company is value-driven." And I said to him, "All companies are value-driven. The real question is whether they are driven by values that are based on external natural laws called principles, because those will govern ultimately in all circumstances anyway."

If you and your people have spent time working on your value system, usually those values will reflect true principles. However, sometimes distortions are introduced from the wider culture (from the media, for example) or a subculture (like an obsession with a musical group) or from a magnetic force (like a powerful emotional event or magnetic personality, such as a powerful boss who has a big ego and a deep agenda in a certain direction), and those distortions can totally throw off your sense of direction and your moral bearings. A common though unspoken value in many companies is greed, which distorts a principle-based pursuit of profitability. And when those distortions happen, you get uprooted. You become a double-minded person, a person who is unstable, and you experience a deep inner sense of vertigo.

Another question that comes my way relates to the age-old argument of relative versus absolute truth. People ask me, "How can you suggest there is such a thing as true north, when it's all relative anyway?"

I give them a three-word test of truth:

1. **UNIVERSAL.** If there are no universal principles, there is no true north, nothing you can depend on. You can forget about the character ethic; just create an image that sells well in the social

and economic marketplace. You end up with business and political systems that operate independent of natural laws like integrity and honesty.

The key to a healthy society is to get the social will, the value system, aligned with correct principles. If you declare your independence from principles, you will have a sick organization with distorted values. For instance, the professed mission and shared values of gang members who pillage and plunder might sound very much like many corporate mission statements, using such words as *teamwork, cooperation, loyalty, profitability, innovation, creativity*. The problem is that their value system is not based on the natural laws of honesty and respect for others.

> *Distortions can totally throw off your sense of direction and your moral bearings. And when that happens, you are uprooted. You become a double-minded person, unstable in all your ways, and you experience a deep inner sense of loss.*

2. TIMELESS. True north is a symbol for bedrock principles—principles that don't change over time. To the degree you move away from the laws of nature and toward what is timely and trendy, your judgment is adversely affected. You acquire distorted notions. You start telling rational lies to explain things. And you move away from the governing Law of the Harvest into social and political rules of success. For example, when we read of people in financial trouble, we often hear sad confessions of overbuilding, overborrowing, and overspeculating, lacking objective feedback, just listening to a lot of internal self-talk. Now, these people have a large debt to pay. They have to work hard to survive, without hope of being healthy, let alone wealthy, for years to come.

The ultimate costs of sacrificing excellence to expediency are high in terms of time and money, reputation, and relationships. Invariably, others are adversely affected when we seek to gratify ourselves in the short term. It's dangerous to be lulled away from natural law. Conscience is the repository of timeless truths and principles, the internal monitor of natural law. About the only thing that hasn't evolved is natural laws and principles—true north on the compass. Science and technology have changed the face of most everything else, but the fundamental laws that govern human nature still apply, as time goes by.

3. **SELF-EVIDENT.** A true principle is self-evident, as in the Declaration of Independence: "We hold these truths to be self-evident." That is, you may try to argue against them, but it's futile. If you try to argue against a principle and find it to be a foolish argument, you know you have a natural law. For instance, consider this principle: "You can't talk yourself out of problems you behave yourself into." The principle is that you cannot produce trust without trustworthiness. Now, try to argue against that idea. Observe people who try to talk themselves out of problems they behave themselves into, or a business that tries to employ public relations as a way out of a problem it behaved itself into.

Principles Ultimately Govern

If your current lifestyle is not in alignment with natural principles, then you may want to trade a values-based map for a principle-centered compass. When you recognize that principles ultimately govern, you might willingly subordinate your values to them and align your roles, goals, plans, and behaviors with them.

However, doing so often takes a crisis: your company's downsizing; your job's on the line; your relationship with the boss goes sour; you lose a major account; your marriage is threatened; your financial problems peak; or you've developed a physical problem because you've neglected diet and exercise. In the absence of such a catalytic crisis, we tend to live in numbed complacency—so busy doing good, easy, or routine things, that we don't even stop to ask ourselves if we're doing what really matters. The good, then, becomes the enemy of the best.

Humility is the mother of all virtues. The humble progress because they willingly submit to and try to live in harmony with natural laws and universal principles. *Courage* is the father of all virtues. We need great courage to lead our lives by correct principles and to have integrity in the moment of choice.

When we set up our own self-generated or socially validated value systems, then develop our missions and goals based on what we value rather than on principles, we tend to become laws unto ourselves, proud and independent. Pride hopes to impress; humility seeks to serve others. Just because we value a thing doesn't mean that having it will enhance our quality of life. No reform in government, business, or education will succeed unless based on true-north principles. Yet, we see leaders who cling to their current style based on self-selected values and bad habits—even as their ship is sinking—when they could be floating safely on the life raft of principles. Nothing sinks people faster in their careers than arrogance. Arrogance shouts, "I know best!" In the uniform of arrogance, we fumble and falter; pride comes and goes before the fall. But dressed in humility, we make progress. As Indiana Jones learned in the classic movie *Indiana Jones and the Last Crusade*, "Only the penitent man will pass."

In pride, we often sow one thing and expect to reap another. Many of our paradigms, and the habits that grow out of them, never produce the results we expect because they are based on illusions, advertising slogans, program-of-the-month training, and personality-based success strategies. A great life can't grow out of illusion. So how do we align our lives with true-north realities that govern quality of life?

Four Human Endowments

As human beings, we have four unique endowments—self-awareness, conscience, independent will, and creative imagination—that not only separate us from the animal world, but also help us distinguish between reality and illusion and align our lives with the laws that govern quality of life.

> › *Self-awareness* enables us to examine our paradigms—the lenses through which see the world—to think about our thoughts, to become aware of our social scripting, and to enlarge the separation between stimulus and response. Self-aware, we can take responsibility for reprogramming or rescripting ourselves out of secondary greatness and toward primary greatness. Many movements in psychology, education, and training are focused on an enlarged self-awareness. Most popular self-help literature also focuses upon this capacity. Self-awareness, however, is only one of our unique endowments.
>
> › *Conscience* puts us in touch with something within us even deeper than our thoughts and something outside of us more reliable than our values. It connects us with the wisdom of the ages and the wisdom of the heart. It's an internal guidance system that allows us to sense when we act or even contemplate acting in a way that's contrary to true-north principles. Conscience is universal. As I have helped companies and individuals develop mission statements, I have learned that what is most personal is most general. No matter what people's religions, cultures, or backgrounds are, their mission statements all deal with the same basic human needs: to live (physical and financial well-being), to

love (social well-being), to learn (mental well-being), and to leave a legacy (spiritual well-being).

› *Independent will* is our capacity to act—the power to transcend our paradigms, to swim upstream, to rewrite our scripts, to act based on principles rather than reacting based on emotions, moods, or circumstances. While environmental or genetic influences may be very powerful, they do not control us. We're not victims. We're not the product of our past. We are the product of our choices. We are *response-able*, meaning we are able to choose our response. This power to choose is a reflection of our independent will.

› *Creative imagination* empowers us to create beyond our present reality. It enables us to write Personal Mission Statements, set goals, plan meetings, or visualize ourselves living with fidelity to principle even in the most challenging circumstances. We can imagine any scenario we want for the future. We can't work on memory alone. Memory is limited. It's finite; it deals with the past. Imagination is infinite; it deals with the present and the future, with potentiality, with vision and mission and goals, with anything that is not now but can be. The man-on-the-street approach to success is to work harder, to give it the so-called old college try. How-

> *As human beings, we have four unique endowments—self-awareness, conscience, independent will, and creative imagination—that not only separate us from the animal world, but also help us to distinguish between reality and illusion, to transform the clock into a compass, and to align our lives with the extrinsic realities that govern quality of life.*

ever, unless willpower is matched with creative imagination, those efforts will be weak and ineffective.

Nurturing Our Unique Gifts

Enhancing these endowments requires us to nurture and exercise them continuously. It's like a meal. Yesterday's meal will not satisfy today's hunger. Last Sunday's big meal won't prepare me for this Thursday's challenges. I will be much better prepared if I meditate every morning and visualize myself dealing with my challenges with authenticity, openness, honesty, and as much wisdom as I can bring to bear on it.

Here are four ways to nurture your unique endowments.

> › **NURTURE SELF-AWARENESS BY KEEPING A PERSONAL JOURNAL.** Keeping a personal journal—a daily in-depth analysis and evaluation of your experiences—is a high-leverage activity that increases self-awareness and enhances all the endowments and the synergy among them.
>
> › **EDUCATE YOUR CONSCIENCE BY LEARNING, LISTENING, AND RESPONDING.** Most of us work and live in environments that are rather hostile to the development of conscience. To hear the conscience clearly often requires us to be reflective or meditative—a condition we rarely choose or find. We're inundated by activity, noise, conditioning, social media, and flawed paradigms that dull our sensitivity to that quiet inner voice that would teach us true-north principles and our own degree of congruency with them.
>
> I've heard people say that they can't win this battle of conscience because expediencies require lies, cover-ups, deceit, or game playing. That's just part of the job, they say.

Indeed, they say that *is* the job. I disagree. I think such rationalization undermines interpersonal trust and trust between organizations.

A life of total integrity is the only one worth striving for. Granted, it's a struggle. Some trusted advisors—agents, accountants, legal counselors—might say, "This will be political suicide," or "This will be bad for our image, so let's cover it up or lie." You may feel that you really are between a rock and a hard place. Still, with a well-educated conscience or an internal compass, you will rarely, if ever, be in a situation where you only have one bad option. You will always have choices. If you wisely exercise your unique endowments, some moral option will be open to you.

So much depends on how well you educate your conscience, your internal compass. Athletes pay the price to discipline their bodies. You've got to do the same with your own conscience regularly. The more internal uncertainty you feel, the larger the gray areas will be. You will always have some gray areas, particularly as you reach the limits of your education and experience.

> *A life of total integrity is the only one worth striving for.*

As you grow, you learn to make those choices based on what you honestly believe to be the right thing to do instead of the most expedient thing.

> **NURTURE INDEPENDENT WILL BY MAKING AND KEEPING PROMISES.** One of the best ways to strengthen our independent will is to make and keep promises. Each time we do, we make deposits in our personal-integrity account—the amount of trust we have in ourselves, in our ability to walk our talk. To build personal integrity, start by making and keeping small promises. Take it a step and a day at a time.

> **DEVELOP CREATIVE IMAGINATION THROUGH VISUALIZA-
TION.** Visualization, a high-leverage mental exercise used
by world-class athletes and performers, may also be used to
improve your quality of life. For example, you might visualize yourself in some circumstance that would normally create discomfort or pain. In your mind's eye, instead of seeing
yourself react as you normally do, see yourself acting on the
basis of the principles and values in your mission statement.
The best way to predict your future is to create it.

Roots Yield Fruits

With the humility that comes from being principle-centered, we can
better learn from the past, have hope for the future, and act with
confidence, not arrogance, in the present. Arrogance is the lack of
self-awareness, blindness, an illusion, a false form of self-confidence,
and a false sense that we're somehow above the laws of life. Real
confidence is anchored in a quiet assurance that if we act based on
principles, our quality of life will improve. It's confidence born of
character and competence. Our security is not based on our possessions, positions, credentials, or on comparisons with others; rather, it
flows from our own integrity to true-north principles.

I confess that I struggle with total integrity and do not always
walk my talk. I find that it's easier to talk and teach than to practice
what I teach. I've come to realize that I must commit to having total
integrity, to be integrated around a set of correct principles.

I've observed that if people never get centered on principles at
some time in their life, they will take the expedient political-social
path to success and let their ethics be defined by the situation. They
will say, "Business is business," meaning they play the game by their
own rules. They may even rationalize major offenses in the name of
business, in spite of having a lofty mission statement.

Only by centering on timeless principles, and then living by them, can we enjoy sustained moral, physical, social, and financial wellness.

Application & Suggestions

> Are you too busy doing good, easy, or routine things instead of what really matters? What is the good in your life that is getting in the way of your best? Write down in your personal journal all of your top priorities in life. Then divide them into A and B priorities. Make a plan to ensure that your A priorities get your highest and best effort.

> Creative imagination empowers us to create our own future. It enables us to visualize ourselves living by a Personal Mission Statement even in the most challenging circumstances. Write down circumstances in which you might be tempted to abandon your mission statement. What do you resolve to do in those circumstances?

> To build personal integrity, start by making and keeping small promises. Take it a step and a day at a time for a week. Record your successes in your personal journal.

CHAPTER 4

STAYING ON TRUE NORTH

Rather than love, than money, than fame, give me truth.

—HENRY DAVID THOREAU

It's one thing to assent to the idea that timeless, universal principles govern our lives; it's another to change the direction of our lives in accordance with principles. Going north is a matter of following the compass, but it's easy to get off the path even if we have a compass. This chapter is about staying on course.

Many people sincerely believe that they are headed in the right direction, equipped with the proper values, principles, and ethics, only to find (usually with the help of objective outside forces or a crisis situation) that they have lost their way or at least have wandered way off base. Distractions and distortions have led them into costly detours and dead ends.

So how do we stay true to the principles of primary greatness?

Over the years, I have used a simple Boy Scout compass to illustrate the concept of true north. When speaking to a group of people who have come from many places, I ask them to close their eyes and point where they think north is, then to open their eyes and look around. Everybody laughs when they see people pointing in all directions.

Three Distortions

How do you stay pointed in the right direction? How do you align people in a real organization—and keep them oriented—so that they're all pointing in the same direction? It's not so easy because of distortions in judgment. I will consider three causes of distortion.

1. **BUILDING (CULTURE).** I've learned that if I go outside, out of what- ever building I'm in at the time, the compass needle shifts a little, indicating the internal environment has slightly distorted the compass reading. In the same way, the cultures surrounding us alter our moral sensibilities, yet we rarely reflect on this. We just assume that our current direction is due north. But when we venture out into nature, we find that the needle was off the mark because of the magnetic pull of the building. The same is true of our behavior. We might be going gradually off course because of a distorted moral culture.

2. **PROJECTOR (SUBCULTURE).** I then put the compass facedown onto an overhead projector to show that the machine also alters the compass reading. That distortion I use as an analogy of the subculture of a particular family, group, team, division, or com- pany. Any powerful or persuasive subgroup can create its own slanted definition of due north.

3. **MAGNET (POWERFUL EMOTIONS, STRONG PERSONALITY, OR COMPELLING PHILOSOPHY).** Next, I take a little magnet and put it right next the compass. I find that I can control the compass needle and make it point any way I want it to. I can make it move

in a circle or jiggle back and forth. I use this as an analogy of how significant emotional events can alter our idea of true north, how an extremely powerful personality with a strong ego can alter our sense of north, or how a compelling philosophy that's well presented can distort our perception.

Any one of these three forces, and any number of other forces, could act as a magnet on the compass indicator pointing north. But there is only one *true* north.

COMBINED FORCES. If and when those three forces—culture, subculture, and personality or philosophy—combine, you will see a major distortion. In fact, you may be headed due south, thinking all the time that you are moving toward true north.

One metaphor for this situation is *vertigo*—a condition of dizziness or giddiness, such as when a pilot of a plane loses orientation and becomes confused. It results in a lack of kinesthetic awareness, a lost sense of where you are in space and where you are in relation to the earth. You may be dealing with a sloping cloud bank, thinking you're level to the earth, only to discover too late that you aren't. Many crashes, both personal and organizational, are caused by ethical vertigo.

Back to Standards

Why are so many individuals and organizations lost? Because there are many seductive messages and forces at play. Many of the media messages directed at us invite us to indulge ourselves without conscience.

People get lost when they use a local norm or internal standard to justify covert or corrupt business practices. The best leaders maintain a sense of humility. They sacrifice their pride and share their power; their influence, both inside and outside their companies, is multiplied because of it.

Humility keeps us in harmony with natural law, which we can't break without harming ourselves. I'm convinced that anyone can handle success or failure, including wealth or fame, as long as he or she has a strong sense of accountability to principles. In the best organizations, natural laws and principles govern—like the constitution of a nation—and even the top people must bow to principle. No one is above it.

When people become laws unto themselves, they essentially represent a magnetic force pointing away from true north, down a pathway of arrogance and defeat.

Normally, the art of politics is the art of getting elected and re-elected. But one U.S. senator was different. He never announced he was going to run for the next election until the last possible hour because he didn't want himself or his staff to trim their sails. He wanted them to stay the course. He was determined to serve his constituents with no thought as to how it would affect his reelection chances.

So I challenge you to go back to your office today or to your family tonight and simply ask the question, "What is our purpose or mission, and what is our primary strategy by which to achieve it?" You might be astonished by the different answers, and you might just begin to see that without alignment behind the same vision, and without leveraging the right principles, everything else gets messed up. You will have a political culture rather than a principled culture, and the type of people you attract will be less principled and more political.

> *Without alignment behind the same vision, and without being tied into the same value system based on principles, everything else gets messed up.*

I assure you that if you get your family or team together in an atmosphere of trust, freedom, and open information, you will come up with the same basic value system, and it will be based on principles: This sense is deeply embedded in everyone's mind.

I invite you to try this in your company. I think you will find that you have a common value system; of course, many differences will be evident. However, if you show respect for each other and seek synergy, you will work through those differences, and begin to regard them as strengths.

Application & Suggestions

› We are surrounded by sources of distraction and distortion that can pull us off our highest and best priorities. Write in your journal: What is a source of distortion in your life? How can you overcome this pull in order to get back to true north?

› What principles or natural laws might you be working against in your life or your business? Record how you will turn this situation around.

› What principle or natural law could you make better use of? Record how you will leverage this principle.

› Go to your office today or to your family tonight and ask the question, "What is our purpose or our mission, and what might be our main strategy for achieving it?" Record the results. Make a short-term plan: What can you do in the next few days to make that mission and strategy a reality?

CHAPTER 5

REPROGRAMMING YOUR THINKING

A person cannot do right in one department
of life while attempting to do wrong in another
department. Life is one indivisible whole.

—GANDHI

Our beliefs about the world determine how we behave. Those beliefs
can act as mental prisons that can keep us from becoming centered
on principles. If we believe secondary greatness is better than primary greatness, we have no hope of achieving primary greatness.
This chapter will help you understand the belief systems that keep
people imprisoned and unable to change. You will also learn how to
break out of those prisons.

As I watched a magnificent sunrise in Hawaii recently from my
hotel window, I thought of a couplet from Dale Carnegie:

Two men looked out from prison bars:
one saw mud, the other saw stars.

What we see in our current circumstance will be greatly influenced by our perspective. Looking down, we may only see mud and bars; or looking up, we may see beams of light from the sun, moon, and stars.

I know many people who feel imprisoned by their roles and their relationships, out of balance and out of sync both at work and at home. The bars that keep them in prison are rarely tangible—there are few, if any, physical barriers or restraints to seeing the stars.

Four Root Causes

So, what's the problem? What keeps us behind bars, seeing mud instead of stars? The problem stems from four roots:

EMOTIONAL IMPRISONMENT. When we disappoint or disagree with another person, we are often labeled and cast into that person's mental prison. We may cross over some sensitive line and hurt, insult, or offend another person. We may feel justified at the time, feeling that the person deserves this treatment. The other person sees it differently, takes offense, builds walls, and locks us up in this prison cell lined with labels. These labels tend to be self-fulfilling prophecies: "He hates me; I can't trust him; he's biased; he's unfair." People tend to become as we treat them, or as we believe them to be. And if others believe those things of you, they will treat you accordingly.

Whenever I cross over the sensitive line out of anger, I wound feelings. My pride, for a while, may keep me from apologizing. The other person is hurt, and the relationship is strained. If I merely try to be better and not confess and ask forgiveness, the other person will still be suspicious. He has been hurt and wounded, so his guard is up. He is defensive, and suspicious of my new behavior. Nothing I can do will change his mind, because I am behind bars and walls in a prison of his own making. These bars and walls are the mental and emotional labels he puts on me.

Thus, we see people sprinting to their cars after work because they're anxious to start their so-called real life. They experience so much terrible management and control in their work life that they want to get out of that stifling environment and into something that's meaningful to them.

SOLUTION: PAY THE PRICE TO GET OUT OF JAIL. It is only by acknowledging my own failings and by seeking forgiveness that I can get out of the jail cell.

THE SICKNESS OF FINDING FAULT. There is a strong universal tendency to find fault in others, to see the microscopic faults of another while ignoring our own major faults. When we focus on the faults in others, we tend to rationalize and justify the faults in our own life. If we then try to correct another person, it doesn't work.

> *Labels tend to be self-fulfilling prophecies. People tend to reflect how we treat them, or as we believe them to be.*

We may be right, but our approach is wrong. We hurt, reject, offend, and threaten. Because of the beam in our eye, we can't see our faults clearly. Our judgment may be entirely wrong. We may be merely projecting our own weakness and calling it his. We may mistake observation for introspection. If we have a self-serving motive, that motive will be translated in a thousand negative ways in every aspect of our lives.

SOLUTION: FIRST, WORK ON YOURSELF. The first step we take in improving any situation is to work on our own personal faults. If we remove our own faults, we then will see clearly to help others. We then become a light, not a judge. In his book *Take This Job and Love*

It, author Dennis Jaffe advises us to take responsibility and get out of the victim mentality; to learn to confront the issues and either leave the job or make needed changes and love it.

SCARCITY SCRIPTING. People with a Scarcity Mentality believe there is only so much pie to go around; if you get a piece, that's one less piece for me. That leads to win-lose thinking: If you win, I lose, and I can't allow that.

Scarcity thinking comes from several sources: Conditional love supplied at home may cause us to try to win love by good behavior but leaves us without a sense of intrinsic self-worth; comparisons at school and work cause us to develop a comparison-based identity; competition in the family, school, work, sports, and in social life reinforces this Scarcity Mentality. We suffer from scarcity thinking in the following four ways:

› Personally, the scarcity script becomes our life script. It becomes deeply embedded. Even though we are unaware of it, we look at life through this lens, which affects everything we see.
› Interpersonally, this scarcity paradigm gets translated into our marriages and into all relationships at work. When push comes to shove, this scarcity drives us to win-lose thinking in our dealings with customers, suppliers, and everybody else.
› In our leadership roles, we don't want to share our power: We don't want to give the keys to the inmates. We feel that if we start empowering people, we'll have less power.

  It's a self-fulfilling prophecy. If we have a comparison-based identity, we will always see ourselves as deficient. Will we want to share profit or gain? Will we want to share recognition with other people? Will we want to share knowledge?

No, because knowledge, position, recognition, and profit are power.

> Organizationally, the scarcity mindset shows up in win-lose systems. We are the system designers, so we will design structures and systems based on how we see the world. We can hold psych-'em-up company events, but if the system is rigged so that most people lose, everyone becomes cynical and no one really buys in.

SOLUTION: WIN-WIN, ABUNDANCE SCRIPTING. People with an Abundance Mentality see the world differently. They believe there is more than enough pie to go around, and that they can always make more pie. This mentality leads to win-win thinking. A win-lose person will convert a win-win system into win-lose. Only a person with an Abundance Mentality and a win-win style can break the cycle of scarcity and win-lose thinking. When people cultivate an Abundance Mentality, they will think win-win. They will develop more self-respect and respect for others and show tremendous compassion and tenderness toward others. There's no such thing as organizational behavior, only individual behavior.

> *When people cultivate an Abundance Mentality, they will think win-win. They will develop more self-respect and respect for others and show tremendous compassion and tenderness toward others.*

Like most people, I had to grow out of scarcity toward an abundance mindset. What helped me was to develop a great mission and to become more concerned with what is right than with who is right. People can and do change from scarcity to abundance thinking. Gandhi was heavily scripted in timidity, scarcity, fear, and distrust. He was threatened by people; he didn't want to be around them. But when he finally gained a vision of his life's purpose, he was able to subordinate those feelings and lead his people.

ROLE IMBALANCE. Why even try to balance our lives when we play so many roles, all very demanding? If we don't live by the principle of balance, we will crash.

Most people live believing they can get away with losing their balance. That's living a lie. It gets translated in a thousand and one different ways. I agree with what Gandhi said: "A person cannot do right in one department of life while attempting to do wrong in another department. Life is one indivisible whole." You can't ignore your family while you put in eighteen-hour days and expect to have a great family life. You can't fritter away your time on social media without paying a price in terms of your health and productivity. I'm sorry, but reality doesn't work that way.

We are all buffeted by different forces that tend to knock us off balance, especially if we have no sense of purpose. We seek the world we see before us. The key question is this: What do we see—mud or stars?

SOLUTION: FIRST, ACCEPT GRACEFULLY A SEASON OF IMBALANCE, BUT VIEW IT WITH A LONG-TERM PERSPECTIVE. We all move through different phases of life and, while we might wish for a more balanced life at certain times, what really matters is long-term balance. Today's imbalance may be natural and necessary from the perspective of the week, month, or year. Getting an advanced degree takes a few concentrated years. A project at work might require intense focus for a while. However, if your entire life is invested in one role, such as work or study, everything else eventually crashes: family, friendships, health. Still, during times of sacrifice and focus, avoid guilt and take a long-term perspective.

SECOND, INVOLVE PEOPLE IN YOUR MOST MEANINGFUL WORK. I've seen people get so consumed with a truly meaningful project that they neglect everyone and everything else. They leave their family behind. They have no social life, very little recreation, even very few breaks for food or pleasure. And all of this might seem necessary for a while, but if you involve family and friends in the significance of the project, they will feel less neglected. They might even be inspired and uplifted. Involve your family in your work. Let them share in the vision and feel part of the mission. I try to do that. I try to take them with me or involve them significantly in other ways.

THIRD, SHARE A COMMON VISION OF THE DESIRED END RESULT. What would happen if everyone on a tour had a different destination in mind? That's essentially what happens when people are kept in the dark or have incomplete information. Don't leave them to make decisions and act based on an unclear vision. A shared vision of a challenging, meaningful project, goal, or purpose can wash away all petty concerns. People with a great shared purpose will subordinate their egos. They will have one heart, one mind, one voice, because they have to get the job done.

FOURTH, DEVELOP A COMPLEMENTARY TEAM. Start doing more leadership work. Stop managing so much. Most companies and families are overmanaged and underled. Of course, the opposite may also be true—you may be overleading and undermanaging. Both management and leadership are necessary. In my own business, I was heavily into the leadership side, and we reached the point of financial hemorrhaging because I wasn't managing. We had to develop a complementary team of people who were skilled in financial management. Immediately, the team made my strengths more productive and my weaknesses irrelevant. Most of us want to clone people in our own image, but what we really need are people around us who are different from ourselves—who are emotionally independent of us, complement our strengths, and compensate for our weaknesses.

FIFTH, PRESERVE SOME PRECIOUS TIME FOR YOUR DEAREST PEO-PLE AND CAUSES. Every leader struggles with balance. There are so many demands on their time. It's hard for me to do creative work because of the many speeches and events I do, so I rely on my home as a preserve, like a game preserve or a forest preserve, where I can do some creative work or have uninterrupted family time. I preserve these times through long-range planning around prioritized values. I schedule some family activities two years ahead and try to hold them inviolate. It's like putting fences around that time.

SIXTH, MAKE WHAT IS IMPORTANT TO THE OTHER PERSON AS IMPOR-TANT TO YOU AS THE OTHER PERSON IS TO YOU. When I'm at home, I try to give myself to my wife and family. I let them write the agenda. I go on their dates. I do what they want to do. For example, I don't care all that much for golf, but my boy does; therefore, I play golf because I care about him.

When my sons and daughters were growing up, I found that sometimes the best thing I could do was just to be there—not to have any agenda of my own, just to be there with them and for them. After a while, they would start to talk about what they wanted to talk about. But I had to demonstrate that I was there for them not only physically but mentally. Your kids will open up if you open your ears and heart, close your mouth, and be there for them.

Application & Suggestions

> Write in your journal the answers to these questions: Do you ever feel trapped or imprisoned? What keeps you behind bars, seeing mud instead of stars? What is the source of this feeling of being stuck in a rut or unable to move forward?
> Have you been improperly labeled? How did that control your actions? Have you incorrectly labeled someone, in ei-

ther your professional or your personal life? Take one step today, however small, to correct those labels.

› Answer in writing: Are you an abundance thinker? Do you really want to share profits with others? Do you want to share recognition with other people? Do you want to share knowledge? In what ways are you a scarcity thinker? Resolve to find one opportunity for sharing knowledge, credit, and recognition and do it. How does it feel?

› Start doing more leadership work. Stop managing so much. Most companies and families are overmanaged and underled. What one thing can you do today to be a leader rather than a manager?

II

12 LEVERS OF SUCCESS

CHAPTER 6

THE LEVER OF INTEGRITY

If you don't stand for something, you will fall for anything.

—GORDON A. EADIE

Total integrity is the first lever of primary greatness. People who have lost integrity live and work in a world of *seeming to be* something they are not. Living a false life is a heavy burden on your conscience and on the people who rely on you. Total integrity lifts that burden from your life. Those who have primary greatness are people for whom total integrity is deeply inscribed in their character. This chapter is about centering your life on the principle of total integrity.

I think that talking about ethics often takes us down the wrong path. Many people confuse ethics with legal issues, or they take a departmental or compartmental approach to ethics, rather than an integrated and organic approach.

By contrast, with an organic approach to integrity, we naturally see *everything* through an ethical lens; consequently, everything is integrated, not seen in different frames or departments.

Primary greatness is about what *is*; secondary greatness is all about *what seems to be*.

Wrestling with issues of integrity, Shakespeare's Hamlet says, "What a piece of work is a man! how noble in reason! how infinite in faculty! in form and moving how express and admirable! in action how like an angel! in apprehension how like a god!" He counsels, "Suit the action to the word, the word to the action." And he reasons, "What is a man if his chief good and market of his time be but to sleep and feed? a beast, no more. Sure, he that made us with such large discourse, looking before and after, gave us not that capability and godlike reason to fust in us unused." To his mother, the Queen, Hamlet responds, "Seems, madam! nay, it is; I know not 'seems.'"

For people who have lost integrity, *seems* is all they know. They live and work in a world of *seeming to be* something they are not. They worry more about how others see them than about who they are. They are actors who wear a false face to cover up covert operations or maintain an image.

When I was working in North Carolina, I was given a shirt imprinted with the state motto in Latin, *Esse quam videri*, which means "To be rather than to seem."

This should be the motto of every person seeking primary greatness. Unfortunately, too often "seeming to be" substitutes for real integrity. It's "seeming" as opposed to "being."

Two Primary Traits of Integrity

So how do you arrive at integrity?

I see integrity as the child of two primary character traits: humility and courage.

Humility means realizing that, over time, principles ultimately govern. A humble person doesn't say, "I am in control," or "I am in charge of my destiny." That theme, so common in much of the success literature in recent decades, is a product of the social value system. And our social values may not be based on rock-solid principles, but on the shifting sands of ego or opinion.

The president of an international communications firm once showed me his company's values statement: "We are committed to the practice of all praiseworthy values that enhance the worth of individuals and strengthen our communities." When I asked him about his core values, he mentioned: *Integrity, excellence, service, profitability, sensitivity, sincerity,* and *high ethical and moral standards.*

I said, "There's certainly nothing wrong with this set of corporate values, as they are closely aligned with enduring principles. However, what matters most is how you integrate them into your daily operations." I was trying to teach what every employee already knows: *An emphasis on legal, ethical, and moral standards is best made not simply with words on a poster in the corporate office, but with the attitudes and actions of people at all levels.*

> *For people who have lost integrity, seems is all they know. They live and work in a world of seeming to be something they are not. They worry more about how others see them than about who they are. They are actors who wear a false face to cover up covert operations or maintain an image.*

This humble business leader well understood the importance of walking the talk and making sure that the talk—the corporate value system—was based on principles. He realized that we are not in control, that natural laws and principles control, and that the attitude of humility is, in a sense, the mother of all virtues, because all of them come through that spirit of submission to pragmatic reality.

The father of all virtues is courage, because when put to the test, courage defines our commitment to those virtues. Eventually, every value is tested. Whether we will align our values, our lives, and our habits with those principles is the big question. Again, "To be, or not to be," is the big question. Seeming to be is not the question.

In other words, will we really live by our principles? We may be humble, but are we courageous? Will we, in fact, swim upstream against very powerful social values or against our own individual tendencies? Will the chief good and market of our time be but to sleep and feed? Or will we put our "infinite faculty, admirable form, and godlike reason" to good use? We won't if we lack the courage to act upon our core beliefs. In fact, our principle-centered initiatives will likely be rolled over and flattened by the latest wave of trendy social values.

When you have both humility and courage, you naturally develop integrity. Integrity means that your life is integrated around principles and that your security comes from within, not from without. It also means, as my friend suggested, maintaining "the highest levels of honesty and credibility in all relationships."

You won't have integrity if you lack humility, or if you have the humility but lack the courage to act on your conviction. Rather than integrity, you then have duplicity, hypocrisy, or what I call the *personality ethic* rather than the character ethic. People who lack integrity will give you an outward show of personality that isn't anchored in the ethical standards of true character. It's counterfeit. False integrity means your security still lies outside yourself. You are secure only to the degree to which you are accepted by others, and to the degree to which you compare or compete favorably with others.

At the end of my book *The 7 Habits of Highly Effective People,* I confess to the reader that I personally struggle with much of what I have shared, but that the struggle is worthwhile and fulfilling because it gives meaning to my life and enables me to love, to serve, and to try again. The challenge of living with integrity is always in front of me.

I've been in a dialogue with myself all my life because of this. I wonder whether I have the right to teach something I don't always live by. And in the process, I have discovered the truth of something psychologist Carl Rogers once said: "That which is most personal is most general." Most people go through the same internal dialogue.

I have also discovered, as I have entered into this private dialogue with myself, that this secret self is the very battleground from which the insights come. The closer you get to the inner truth of who you really are, the more you get the insights that, ironically, everybody else can relate to.

Economic crises have taught us this lesson. One business after another has been humbled in recent years. The financial industry stumbled because of practices that did not always demonstrate integrity. Many great companies have been brought down by a lack of humility and awareness of the realities of what they were doing. And some have gone through some deep soul searching.

Many of us are coerced into humility, but it's better to humble ourselves by choice. As we develop more internal security and integrity, we will then be humbled by conscience, not by circumstance, not by force.

If we don't take account of ourselves and use our self-knowledge, we'll always be projecting our motivations onto the outside world. With our limited vision, we think we see the world. We mistake observation for introspection. We misunderstand ourselves, other people, and the world if we are constantly in a state of projection and observation. We must pay the price through honest introspection to gain self-knowledge.

Three Selves in One

Each of us is a composite of three selves: the public self (our public image and persona), the private self (what we do in our own private world of family and close associates when we let our hair down), and our deep, secret self (our inner self where we can examine the scripts of our lives—our motivations, tendencies, and habits rooted in our genetic coding, our environment, and our social conditioning). Integrity arises—or fails to—from that deep, secret self.

Most people try to exercise influence through an outside-in approach, based in their public selves. However, people who are highly effective exercise influence through an Inside-Out Approach based in their secret selves. If you reveal authentically who you are deep down, people will learn to trust you for your genuineness.

As you come to know yourself better and become open to influence at the private and secret levels, you are in a better position to influence others because they'll sense that you are open to influence, open to feedback, and they'll be more open themselves. The primary reason you have more influence with others is that you first know yourself.

Great minds have taught "know thyself," "control thyself," and "give thyself," and I would emphasize that there is power in that sequence.

For example, suppose I hear a rumor that you are saying and doing things to hurt me. By exercising self-knowledge, I might say to myself, "Now, before you overreact to this news, remember, Stephen, that you have this paranoid tendency to think people are against you. Don't interpret what people are saying in terms of that paranoia. Instead, go to them and get additional data."

Now, notice what happens. When I take into account my paranoid tendency and get additional data, I often find that my fears are unfounded. And if I have integrity, I can say to you, "I'm very upset, but I'm trying to deal with this in a responsible way and not overreact emotionally." I'm taking responsibility for myself. I'm using self-knowledge. I'm not attacking you on the basis of a rumor. Thus, when you and I interact, I can allow you to influence me.

Legendary psychologist Carl Rogers says that when we feel that our internal congruency is disturbed, we use various psychological defenses such as denial, intellectualization, rationalization, or projection. Projection happens when I project my own motivations onto other people. We judge others by their behavior, ourselves by our intentions.

I took part in an experiment in Bethel, Maine, where researchers performed a psychological dissonance study on a group of us to identify what defense mechanisms we tend to use when push comes to shove in our lives. They identified those who used intellectualization as a defense mechanism, those who used rationalization, those who used denial, and those who used projection. They put us into groups of people of the same ilk, then gave us tasks to perform.

My defense mechanism was intellectualization. You can imagine what my group was like. We were a bunch of academics who had chosen our profession partly because it was safe. We could escape into our minds and into theoretical abstractions. Well, we were assigned this task to do together, but we couldn't move it forward at all. We suffered from the paralysis of analysis.

In another room, those in the projection group were all transferring their own motivations onto each other. They got into blaming each other, and they got bogged down too.

The people in the denial group couldn't move forward either, because everyone was saying, "Oh, no, that's not what the assignment means. They don't really want us to do that."

This experiment taught me again the importance of examining

my own motives and methods for dealing with hard problems. I was reminded of how easy it is for me to fall into the trap of intellectualizing away my responsibility for my own life. You might be using other defense mechanisms to fall into the same trap.

Our influence with others increases only to the degree with which we have internal and external congruency. I once witnessed this dynamic in action when a friend, who had offended me deeply, apologized to me. I said to him, "I can't tell you how much I admire that sincere apology. How did you reach the point where you could do that?" And he said, "I had to go deep within myself and carry on a personal dialogue. I carried on the dialogue to the point where I had enough self-knowledge that I could ask myself, 'What am I going to obey—my ego or my conscience?'" Then he said, "I decided to obey my conscience."

My friend is such a conscience-directed person that, if he gets into a battle with his ego, he'll go with his conscience every time because he's done it so often. Listening to his conscience is an ingrained habit with him. He has great influence with others because of his integrity.

Many people have an internal dialogue, but they lack the courage to confess an error or to apologize or make the change in public. Courage is a function of integrity. If we don't cultivate integrity over time, we won't have the courage to confess mistakes and correct course.

The Fruits of Integrity

Integrity produces unquestionable benefits in your life.

> › One child of integrity is *wisdom*. If your security comes from within, you simply have better judgment. You're not

in an overreactive state; you don't dichotomize; you don't catastrophize; you're not extreme. You have better overall life balance. With wisdom, you see things in correct perspective and proportion; you don't overreact or underreact. You "suit the action to the word, the word to the action," as Shakespeare wrote.

> A second child of integrity is the *Abundance Mentality*. When you get your security from within, you are not in a constant state of comparison from without. Therefore, you can have an abundance mindset toward life. You stop worrying about others getting more credit or having more success in life. You see life as an ever-enlarging cornucopia of resources that gets larger and larger. As Hamlet said, "There is nothing either good or bad, but thinking makes it so." In the same way, if you look for scarcity, that's what you'll get. If you look for the abundant, perhaps hidden, resources all around you, you'll be able to leverage those resources.

> A third child of integrity is *synergy*. When your security is not tied up with what other people think of you, you can work with them to come up with better ideas in a spirit of win-win. You can express your ideas with courage and consideration with the intent of finding the best possible alternative, not simply to get credit for the best idea.

> Another sweet fruit of personal and organizational integrity is *relationships of trust with all stakeholders*. You simply can't have integral relationships without genuine personal integrity. Many bottom-line business benefits—including competitiveness, flexibility, responsiveness, quality, economic value added, and customer service—depend on relationships of trust. At bottom, only people with integrity are trustworthy.

Corporate Ethics Programs

With so much riding on integrity and ethics, why are breaches in ethics, both individual and corporate, all too common?

For years now we've seen a heavy emphasis on ethics training in colleges and in organizations.

Organizations spend lots of money on ethics programs. Sadly, according to one recently retired ethics director, "Some executives are concerned primarily with public image and perceptions. In fact, the ethics program is often started as a response to public outcry or internal inquiry. Ethics directors serve as a point of contact for whistleblowers and for unempowered and uninformed individuals who don't know how else to get a problem resolved. When leaders justify the means by the ends, people pick up the signals. They note who is hired, promoted, and rewarded—and why. They see who gets away with murder and who condones inappropriate behavior. Having an ethics program may make people more sensitive to such issues as sexual harassment or sexist language, but they rarely stop or even slow the avalanche of unethical behavior. In fact, the program may just drive unethical behavior further underground, making people even more devious."

To work at looking ethical is a fundamentally flawed approach, because it's not about humility—accepting principles, aligning with those principles, submitting to them, and obeying them. It's more about pride—having some compartment inside a person or an organization called ethics or values, but not deeply integrated.

As universities and corporations add classes or offices dealing with ethics, people begin to see issues through that departmental frame of reference rather than having their perspectives governed by a universal frame of reference—a framework of integrity through which they see everything.

The ethics dilemma is analogous to the quality dilemma. You

can't have a so-called department of quality and think you've done the job. You can't add quality to a product after it is finished; rather, you have to design and build it in from the beginning, seeing everything you do through the lens of quality. Likewise, you can't inspect in ethics. When everybody accepts personal responsibility to behave in ethical ways, you hardly have to think about it, because ethical behavior is your nature, not the responsibility of some artificial department down the hall.

> When leaders justify the means by the ends, people pick up the signals. They note who is hired, promoted, and rewarded—and why. They see who gets away with murder and who condones inappropriate behavior.

When leaders are open and exact in their observance of ethical codes, they inspire others to do the same. One leader, when stepping down as president of a large university, was commended by the chairman of the board: "A few reach the pinnacle of professional or social or financial success through devious means. Others may be more virtuous but still show a lack of sensitivity to loved ones, friends, and colleagues as they climb to the top. Those who combine honor, integrity, devotion, and sensitivity to family and friends are rare indeed. You are one of the rare ones."

Too often ethics are separate from the everyday life of the organization. Professional ethicists may huddle and talk, but most of their practice is reactive in response to people not walking their talk, feeling that the only wrong is in getting caught. They may handle a complaint to allay a lawsuit, but they are not preventative or integrative.

As long as there is a great disparity between the corporate ethical stance and individual behavior, the individual will feel no obligation to live by corporate ethical codes.

Your vision, mission, ethics, and values statements will be even more valuable if you don't rush the creative process, announce the result, then ignore or dismiss the document as some meaningless formal exercise. As you involve people in the creation of a code of ethics and review it regularly with them, you build humility and courage into the culture.

The ethics statement becomes a constitution when it becomes the center from which everything else flows. Then you don't have this "seeming to be ethical." In organizations of integrity, ethics is not just another department. The organization serves as a second family. People are humble because they know that principles are in control, not people, programs, and politics. They not only believe in timeless principles, but also have the courage to act on them.

Application & Suggestions

> Write in your journal: What does it mean to you to be a person of total integrity? Choose one area in your life in which you could show more integrity, then do it. How does it feel?
> In what areas of your life are you an example of courage? of humility? To what extent do you enjoy the fruits of integrity in your life now? Write down one circumstance in which you could have shown more courage and another circumstance in which you could have shown more humility. Try it.

CHAPTER 7

THE LEVER OF CONTRIBUTION

Look around you. There is not a life in this room that you have
not touched, and each of us is a better person because of
you. We are your symphony, Mr. Holland. We are the melodies
and the notes of your opus. We are the music of your life.

—MR. HOLLAND'S OPUS

Primary greatness is achieved by those who have a mission, a purpose to serve that is higher than themselves, a lasting contribution
to make. Many of us are tempted to take the easy way through life,
never asking much of ourselves, and never ask the liberating ques-

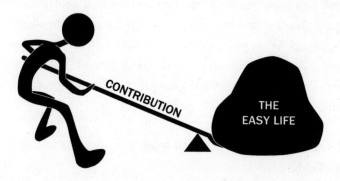

tions, "What does the world need from me? How can I contribute to the lives of others?" This chapter will help you think deeply about the legacy you want to leave.

I was once asked at the height of a period of economic dislocation, "What do you think about the massive layoffs that are taking place?"

My response: "This is just one episode. As we move toward the global economy and the new rules that govern the workplace, we'll see more competition from high-quality and low-cost producers, and this competition will exceed anything we have known in the past, particularly as we see the emergence of Asian, South American, Indian, Chinese, and Middle Eastern economies."

As the psychological contract with people at work is revised around the world, many individuals will get into accusatory modes—into blaming organizations, societies, or governments for their problems.

Personal Redesign

Rather than place blame, these people need to reconsider their own purposes and redesign themselves to accommodate the new reality. I'm thinking of three things in particular.

THEY NEED A SENSE OF WHAT TRUE NORTH IS TO THEM. They must define a personal mission based on a vision that contributes to the organization and a value system that is principle-centered, that will not change. Otherwise, they'll be buffeted by all these powerful forces and megatrends, and they'll end up being reactive—blaming others for their problems and losing their influence over their own future.

THEY MUST BE WILLING TO BEAR RISK. They must be willing to take three kinds of risk:

> *In the way they speak.* They need to show not only consideration but also *courage* in the way they speak to their bosses, their co-workers, and other stakeholders.
> *In the way they listen.* They need to listen with empathy to learn what's happening in the organization, even though the information might disrupt their world view.
> *In the way they act.* They must be willing to bear the risk of being creative, of teaching, and of leaving their comfort zone, so that they can adapt to the new reality and experiment to determine if there are new ways of doing things that work better. Risk taking will be the prime characteristic of the leaders of the future. In a sense, everybody must get into business for themselves and become entrepreneurs. They might move around within network organizations or massive matrix organizations from one project to another—and they've got to add value each time they have a new assignment. People are less focused on lifelong careers with one organization; they must become more focused on getting a job done, on meeting needs, on adding value, and on documenting the value they add.

THEY MUST MAKE AND KEEP A COMMITMENT TO LIFELONG LEARNING. People must accept the personal responsibility to upgrade their knowledge and skills, to become more and more tech-savvy, to read widely, and to become aware of the powerful forces that are operating in their environments. They may need to gain or regain a liberal or fine-arts education, in addition to keeping up on what is happening in the world of technology and science, because the arts increase the capacity of the mind to keep learning. They also need to develop a value system that supersedes technology and science, so that they live well with the internal side of their nature.

Those who do these three things will find that their influence will expand far beyond their immediate vision and beyond their business and their family, their children, and their community. They will make the great contributions they are capable of making.

Artistic Leaders and Followers

To achieve line of sight between what the world needs and what you offer, you need to answer three questions: *What does the world need? What am I good at? How can I best do what I like to do and meet real needs where I now work?* In effect, you must become an artistic leader and follower.

The classic movie *Mr. Holland's Opus* makes a powerful statement about the need to be an artist of life. Mr. Holland is an aspiring composer who takes a temporary job teaching music in a high school. He hates the job at first; it has nothing to do with his aspirations in life. But months turn into years, and in time he develops a love for his students. His life's work—his opus—turns out to be not a great musical composition, but a great contribution to the lives of thousands of young people. It is a contribution of the soul.

> *To achieve line of sight between what the world needs and what you offer, you need to answer three questions:*
> *What does the world need?*
> *What am I good at?*
> *How can I best do what I like to do and meet real needs where I now work?*

People have a hunger today for the soul side of life—a hunger created in part by our turning away from the fine arts in recent decades. I once visited a great private school that was built on a strong STEM (science, technology, engineering, math) foundation. They are moving into the fine arts as well as mathematics and science. They have come to an understanding of the need for emotional intelligence—

the need to nurture other dimensions of our natures they had undervalued.

The new workers, the new worker-leaders, and the new leader-workers will seek both intellectual and emotional intelligence and focus on adding value, continuous learning, building relationships of trust, and centering on timeless principles. It's a renaissance education that leads to a renaissance in organizations.

Two Sides of Leadership

THE FIRST SIDE IS THE PRIVATE VICTORY. Many people resist personal transformation, even when they know it is the right thing to do. Thus, they miss half the story of what it takes to become a leader—the Private Victory.

The Private Victory is the victory over self. You cannot hope to lead others until you can lead your own life with integrity and manage yourself with discipline.

Why do so many people forfeit the Private Victory? I can think of four reasons.

> They transfer the responsibility for their lives to others or to their environment.
> Few people, perhaps only 5 to 10 percent, pay the price and take the time to develop a defined personal mission, philosophy, or creed.
> Many of those who have a personal vision and mission don't pursue it, because it entails risk and effort, and it throws them out of their comfort zone. They abandon it to pursue lesser priorities.
> They currently don't have the mindset or skillset for it, and the paradigm of lifelong learning is not deeply imbedded in their family or corporate culture. Thus, they never

achieve the Private Victory that makes the Public Victory much more likely.

THE OTHER SIDE OF THE LEADERSHIP STORY IS TO WIN THE PUBLIC VICTORY. The Public Victory is to get others to join you in the quest to achieve a shared vision. Why do so many peak-performing individuals fail this test? I suggest three reasons.

> › Even if they have personal security, they don't have a shared security with a spouse or partner. They want to move out to open sea but are anchored in the harbor.
> › They haven't learned to delegate. Many people know the mechanics of delegation, but they resist delegating fully because they don't want to cede control. They don't want other people taking credit. They don't trust that the job will be done right. I have great empathy for these people; in expanding our company, I have had to make disclosures that were hard for me to make at the time.
> › They fail to involve other people in creating a supportive environment. They don't build a culture to make their vision happen; instead, they sit and blame their managers and others, making the situation worse.

In many respects, Mr. Holland was an entrepreneur who learned, over time, to involve others and build a supportive team. At key times, his willing followers and supporters got behind him to pull off a public parade and program.

If you're ever going to hear your opus played, you'll have to undergo personal redesign and win both the Private and Public Victories, ultimately gaining a shared sense of mission.

Retire or Renew?

Once I was working with a company that was doing well but would need to be reinvented in the near future to meet new challenges. The man in charge was sixty-three, and planned to retire at sixty-five.

As he started to invest effort and energy into this reinvention, he realized that it was a big job, one he could not finish neatly in a couple of years. He wondered why he should even take on the challenge, since he was addressing the needs of tomorrow, and the company was doing well today.

He had to go through his own personal struggle with the question, "Do I have the commitment and the energy to give to this effort, knowing that I only have two years before I retire?"

On the positive side, he felt that the effort would have a cultural impact and would position the company for profitable growth well into the next century. On the downside, he knew the initiative would introduce new problems and risk. And he faced nagging questions: "Will this change really work? How will it impact our culture?"

As I talked to him, I could see that he was struggling: "Should I go in this direction, where I know we need to go? The commitment and energy involved are so tremendous. Or should I stay the conservative course, knowing that my successor will have to deal with all the tough issues?"

I asked him, "What kind of a legacy do you want to leave when you retire?"

And he said, "Well, I don't know. I haven't really thought about that."

I told him, "There are two options you might consider. One is that you make this effort to reinvent this organization; the other is that you stay the course and go out in glory, but without doing what needs to be done to benefit the next generation."

He thought about what I said. The next day when we visited he said, "I have never been asked such a sobering question: What legacy do I want to leave? The more I looked inside my heart, I had to acknowledge that I didn't want to pay the price of this major initiative; in fact, I secretly hoped that I could retire in glory and that my successor wouldn't do as well as I have done. I wanted my tenure to be the highlight. But the more I thought about it, the more I realized that my motive was wrong and that I needed to make the effort so that the company would do even better after I retire."

> *If you're ever going to hear your opus played, you'll have to undergo personal reengineering and win both the Private and Public Victories, ultimately gaining a shared sense of mission.*

He knew this restructuring would take a tremendous commitment on his part. "I hoped for two years of comfort and farewell speeches praising my name," he told me. "Instead, I face the toughest struggle I've ever gone through. But I've concluded that I cannot live with myself unless I make the effort to leave an enduring legacy."

Search Your Own Heart

When this chief executive told me about this internal struggle, I thought of the statement in Psalms: "Search your own heart with all diligence, for out of it flow the issues of life."

That is essentially what he did. He made the leap from self-obsession to contribution. He made the leap from taking the easy way to making a contribution. During this period of reflection, he was extremely honest and authentic with himself and with others. And in the end, he concluded courageously, "I'm willing pay this price. I know this decision will make the next two years much more challenging, but also more rewarding."

I invite you to search your own heart as you ask yourself this question: What legacy will I leave? What will my contribution be? Such searching often stirs up reinvention, redesign, and restructuring because you realize that you must pay the price for profitable growth.

The restraining forces are very real. In fact, as soon as you decide to launch a major change effort, you will find many convincing reasons for why you need not pay the price. Here are but a few of the ready-made excuses that may occur to you.

> The issues you must face are politically sensitive. Just as many politicians put off dealing with issues that are politically sensitive or even potentially suicidal, why shouldn't you do the same?

> The big problem you face is chronic, but it may have no acute manifestations. Why not put the problem on the back burner and leave it there?

> There is no near-term payoff. Why tackle a tough problem that has no near-term payoff? If you play the game right, you could get all the golden eggs in the near term, even though you may endanger the life of the goose.

> Your successor in your job may be a convenient scapegoat. If the change effort you have in mind doesn't work, you have many people and other variables to blame, including your poor successor.

> You have already paid a dear price to be where you are today, so why not let somebody else step up? You deserve to take it easy.

The problem with succumbing to one or more of these ready-made reasons for not tackling the tough issues is that deep down inside your heart, you know "I never really paid the price." And you have to live with that knowledge.

A great challenge frees you to say no to a lot of things. You might find extraordinary psychological relief in taking on the big task and leaving behind the trivial. Often we find it hard to say no to the relatively unimportant issues we face in life and in business unless we have a compelling *yes*—some mission to serve, some quest to undertake, some goal to meet, some legacy to leave.

In my experience, the key to paying the price is to ask the penetrating question regarding your legacy and to reflect deeply in your heart and soul. During this period of deep reflection and introspection, you might involve a few other people for whom your legacy is relevant.

When you resolve to tackle the tough problems and undertake a major change initiative—whether it's personal and private, or public and organizational—you still need the strength to see the thing through. You begin to address and solve problems that may have plagued you or your organization for years. You finally face what must be done to get your act together.

This lesson in soul-searching pertains to anything you might want to do in your life. It's basically a reaffirmation of the idea that Public Victories flow out of Private Victories.

And so I again ask the question, "What legacy do you want to leave?"

Application & Suggestions

> To become an artistic leader and follower, answer these questions: What does the world need from you? What are you good at? How can you best do what you like to do and meet real needs where you now work? Make one goal to pursue in which all of these things come together: a need area, your own talents, and your current reality.

› Answer in writing: What legacy do you want to leave in your personal and professional life? What do you want people to say about you after you leave your current job? What do you want your family and friends to say about you ten years from now?

CHAPTER 8

THE LEVER OF PRIORITY

The key is not to prioritize what's on your schedule,
but to schedule your priorities.

—STEPHEN R. COVEY

Shifting from secondary to primary greatness means that things we too often put first in our lives should actually be last. Some things are just plain more important than others; in fact, some things are so important—your life, your health, your family—that others are trivial by comparison. If your days are filled with "fatal distractions" such as trivial work tasks, gaming, and endless entertainment, you need to

press on the lever of true priorities. This chapter is about discerning the difference between first things and secondary things and making sure that first things *stay* first things.

When my daughter Jenny was preparing for her wedding, I visited her, expecting to find her happy. Instead, I found her frustrated.

She told me, "I have so many other projects and interests that are important to me. But right now, I have to put everything else on hold. I'm spending all my time just preparing for this wedding. I can't even find time to be with my soon-to-be husband."

Seeking to understand, I replied, "So this wedding is consuming you?"

She continued, "I have other work to do. I have other people and projects that need my attention."

I asked her, "What does your conscience tell you to do? Maybe right now, your marriage is the one thing that matters most."

She showed me her to-do list. "I schedule time to do these other things, but then I'm constantly distracted by wedding things."

I told her, "You're doing what matters most to you at this time. So forget your other plans for a few weeks. Relax and enjoy this great event in your life."

"But what about life balance?" she asked, knowing that I teach this principle.

"Your life is going to be unbalanced for a time, and it should be. The long run is where you go for balance. For now, don't even try to keep a schedule. Just enjoy yourself, and let others feel your joy. You won't get much satisfaction from staying on schedule if you have to sacrifice first things and best things. Maybe the only role that matters this entire month will be your role as a new bride. And if you fulfill that role well, you will feel satisfied."

Identify Your First Things

What are the first things in your life? One good way to answer that question is by asking others: "What is unique about me? What are my unique gifts? What is it I can do that no one else can do?" For instance, who else can be a father to your child? a grandparent to your grandchildren? Who else can teach your students? Who else can lead your company? Who else can be a bride to your groom?

Your unique talents and capabilities determine the important work you have to do in life. The tragedy is that our unique contribution is often never made because the important first things in our lives are choked out by other urgent things. Thus, some important works are never started or finished.

In my book *First Things First*, coauthored with Roger and Rebecca Merrill, we suggest that the path to personal effectiveness is a balancing process. We invite people to think through this process very carefully. "What are my responsibilities in life? Who are the people I care about?" The answers become the basis for thinking through your roles. Your goals are then set by asking, "What is the important future state for each relationship or responsibility?"

Setting up Win-Win Agreements with people and maintaining relationships of trust is not an efficient process; in fact, the process is usually slow. However, once trust is in place, the work will go faster. If you're efficient up front, you might be taking the slowest approach. Yes, it might seem more efficient to drum your decision down someone else's throat, but whether or not he or she is committed to live by that decision and to carry it out is a different matter. When dealing with people, slow is fast; fast is slow.

Peter Drucker makes the distinction between a quality decision and an effective decision. You can make a quality decision, but if you don't commit to it, you won't be effective. There has to be commitment to make a quality decision effective. You may be highly efficient working with things, but highly ineffective working with people.

Efficiency is different from *effectiveness*: *Effectiveness* is a results word; *efficiency* is a process word. Some people can climb the ladder of success very efficiently, but if it's leaning against the wrong wall, they won't be effective. You can work very efficiently on the wrong priorities.

Efficiency is about working with *things*. You can move things around fast, you can move money around, you can manage resources, you can manage cash flow, you can rearrange your office furniture. But if you try to be efficient with people on important issues, you'll likely be ineffective.

We can't deal with people as though we're dealing with things. We can be efficient with things, but we need to be effective with people. Have you ever tried to be efficient with a family member or close friend on a tough issue? How did it go?

If you go fast with people, you'll make very slow progress. You won't hear what they're really telling you. You won't understand what a win is for them. If you go slowly and get deeply into win-win thinking, you'll find that, in the long run, it's faster to get commitment to the right resolution for both of you.

> *Our unique contribution is often never made because the important first things in our lives are choked out by other urgent things. And so some important works are never started or finished.*

Effectiveness applies to you as much as to other people. You should never be efficient with yourself either. For example, one morning I met with some people who were creating Personal Mission Statements for themselves. Someone said, "Creating a Personal Mission Statement is a tough process." And I said, "Well, are you approaching it through an efficiency paradigm or an effectiveness paradigm? If you use the efficiency approach, you may try to bang it out this weekend. But if you use the effectiveness approach, you'll keep this dialogue going until you feel at peace."

Subordinate Clock to Compass

For many people, the dominant metaphor of life is still the clock. We value the *clock* for its speed and efficiency. The clock has its place and efficiency has its place, but only *after* you've achieved effectiveness. The symbol of effectiveness is the *compass*, because it provides direction—purpose, vision, perspective, and balance. Like a compass, your conscience serves as an internal monitoring and guidance system every minute of your life.

To move from a clock mindset to a compass mindset, you focus on priorities instead of schedules. The clock can tell you when a meeting is going to be held, but it won't tell you if the meeting is worth going to. What if the meeting diverts you from the path you know you should be on? Each day, each week, be clear on your true-north priorities so you can stay on course.

Keep First Things First

Why do people find it easy to schedule and keep appointments with others, but hard to keep appointments with themselves? If you can make and keep promises to yourself, you will significantly increase your social integrity. If you can make and keep promises to others, you will gain the higher self-discipline to keep promises to yourself.

Of course, you shouldn't overreact if you fail. But keeping promises to yourself increases your integrity enormously.

For example, I once saw my son rebuking his little sister for rearranging his room. He had everything laid out to work on a project, but she thought the room was messy and wanted to help her brother.

In the middle of his tirade, he caught himself and said, "I apologize. I'm just taking my frustrations out on you, and I know you meant well." He apologized right then, in the heat of the moment.

Knowing that people are more important than things, and that relationships are more important than schedules, you can subordinate a schedule without feeling guilty because you superordinate the conscience, the commitment to a larger vision and set of values. When your projects are worthy ones, then your higher purpose will transcend petty concerns and matters of secondary importance.

I recommend this time-management credo: *I will not be governed by the efficiency of the clock; I will be governed by the compass of my conscience.*

As you build your trust levels at work, you decide daily and hourly to do what's necessary at that time. If family needs you, you're there. If you are in an extremely productive or creative phase, you don't let anything interrupt. Can you imagine a doctor taking a telephone call in the middle of surgery?

Most of us are buried in urgency symbolized by the buzzing texts and ringtones that fill our lives. Most jobs call for quick actions that are both urgent and important, but don't confuse urgency with importance. It takes real leadership to act on what is important but not necessarily urgent. The net effects of a reactionary, urgency lifestyle are stress and burnout.

One way to stay focused on the important is to plan your week before you plan your day. Weekly planning affords you a longer-term perspective, enabling you to act within the context of your mission, roles, and goals.

Have a Burning Yes

The highest work any of us will ever do is the creative work we are capable of—the contribution only we can make. However, too many of us sacrifice creative contribution for activities that are far less rewarding and important.

Many times I have said, "You have to decide what your highest priorities are and have the courage—pleasantly, smilingly, unapologetically—to say no to other things. And the way you do that is by having a bigger *yes* burning inside. The enemy of the best is often the good."

From my experience in working with executives and others who are expected to do creative and innovative work, I find that their ability to deliver often comes down to a practical question: "Where am I going to get time and resources to do this sort of work?" Much of the training in creativity and investment in innovation goes down the drain because most people don't know how to make or take time for creative work.

Thus, they lose their creative freedom—the freedom to do their best work and make their highest contribution. They may enjoy great physical liberty, having many options and amazing mobility in their physical environment, but enjoy very little freedom, which is the internal power and discipline to exercise their options wisely. In effect, they become self-proclaimed victims of the clock, and start blaming it for their lack of productivity. The circumstances and conditions of their lives become dominant driving forces. When other people do not come through for them—when cases and fires flare out of control because people neither prevent them nor attend to them—they blame those people and say, "They have caused all my misery."

You won't be very creative when your energy is sapped and your mind is occupied by pressing, urgent concerns. You can't be creative when you are defensive!

Six Safeguards

So how do you safeguard your creative freedom? Here are six principles and practices.

JUST SAY NO: NEGLECT WHAT IS URGENT BUT NOT IMPORTANT. I find that if we neglect what is urgent but not important and attend to what is important but not urgent, we can escape a chronic state of crisis and do more creative work. Busyness is the essence of management. Creativity is the essence of leadership.

Research done on companies that have won the Deming Prize, one of the most coveted quality awards, indicates that the top priority for these companies is economic performance *over time*.

What do these companies do differently? In Deming companies, top executives spend at least 60 percent of their time on true priorities: things that are important but not necessarily urgent, such as preparation, prevention, mission building, planning, relationship building, creation, recreation, and empowerment.

In other companies, executives spend 50 or 60 percent of their time doing things that are urgent but not important, which is the very opposite of what they should do.

The best companies focus on the things that matter most, the things that are important but not necessarily urgent. They don't define importance *as* urgency. Because urgent things require action now, we tend to believe that they are important; as philosopher and educator Charles E. Hummel said, "The appeal of these demands seems irresistible, and they devour our energy. But in the light of eternity their momentary prominence fades. With a sense of loss we recall the important tasks that have been shunted aside. We realize that we've become slaves to the tyranny of the urgent."[9]

Many people tell me, "But you don't know my situation. I have so many balls in the air." Actually, it is very liberating for these people to learn that they can neglect urgent, less important demands with very little impact.

KEEP THAT INTERNAL *YES* BURNING INSIDE. It's much easier to say no to the urgent and the unimportant when you have a burning *yes* to occupy you. If you have a passion for creative work that promises much greater rewards, you can easily say no to less important tasks without experiencing guilt. You can say no courteously, with a smile, feeling free of shame, to the busy work others may demand from you.

> *Executives in the best companies focus on the things that matter most, the things that are important but not necessarily urgent. They don't define importance as urgency.*

One purpose of learning is to distinguish between the important and the unimportant. This judgment requires you to develop criteria for the use of your time that are so deeply embedded that you can say with certainty, "Wait, I won't deal with that issue even though it is urgent and pressing. It's just not important enough." I can't tell you the difference this principle has made in my life!

EARN THE CONFIDENCE OF YOUR BOSS IN YOUR CREATIVE COMPETENCE. When you start saying, "I don't have the freedom to be creative," that becomes your creative challenge: to gain that freedom by building your relationship with your boss and with people who influence your boss.

I'm frequently asked, "What if you think something is less important, but your boss thinks it's very important?" My response to that question is this: *What is important to another person must be as important to you as the other person is to you, or as the common cause between you.* So even though you think it's a less important activity and not worthy of your attention, if the relationship is important to you, and the cause you are working for is important to you, then the task must be important to you.

"Well," you say, "my boss won't support me." Then your creative task is to build your boss's confidence in you so that, gradually, you are allowed to do a little more creative work. If your efforts pay dividends, you will inevitably find yourself free to do more.

BALANCE CREATIVE COURAGE WITH CONSIDERATION FOR OTHERS. Even if you work in a political milieu, if you show the courage of your convictions, you will have a greater degree of freedom than you previously thought possible. Goethe said it most aptly, "Boldness has genius and magic in it." With courage, you can often carry the day. Unless you are bold with others, either you won't get their attention, or they won't sense the depth of your drive and commitment, so you stay at their mediocre level of expectation.

You've got to be proactive and take initiative. At the same time, I define *maturity* as "courage balanced with consideration." This definition wonderfully applies to creativity as well. If you have both courage and consideration, you will be creative. In his book *Motivation and Personality*, Abraham Maslow teaches that the self-actualizing person brings courage and creativity together.

OPERATE IN BOTH A HIGHLY INDEPENDENT MODE AND A HIGHLY IN-TERDEPENDENT MODE. At the core of *The 7 Habits of Highly Effective People* lies the Maturity Continuum, a developmental path moving from dependence to independence to interdependence. This same continuum also applies to creativity. Those creative talents who stop at independence are usually those who burn out early. They're shooting stars. They don't have endurance because they don't build an interdependent team around themselves.

I find that highly creative work is too difficult to endure the market forces unless we have an interdependent mindset and skillset.

With no backup, no relief, no synergy, our strengths become our undoing; our weakness becomes evident because it is not being covered by the strengths of others.

Build a team around yourself of people who can compensate for your weaknesses and let you do what you do best. Peter Drucker once stated, "Build on strengths; organize to make weaknesses irrelevant."

GET OUT OF THE BOX, PUT ON DIFFERENT HATS, AND ENGAGE IN LATERAL THINKING. You may need to follow the advice of Edward de Bono in his classic book *Six Thinking Hats*: "Unscramble your thinking so that you can use one thinking mode at a time—instead of trying to do everything at once." Try thinking creatively without thinking critically. Think logically without thinking optimistically, and so forth. His lateral thinking involves escaping from the usual patterns of thought to new patterns in order to generate new ideas and break out of conceptual prisons. Peter Ueberroth, organizer of the highly successful Los Angeles Olympics, once said it was lateral thinking that turned the games from an event no city wanted to an event for which cities now compete vigorously.

One Week at a Time

As you look back on your life, you may realize that the things that mattered most were too often at the mercy of things that mattered least, that the good was the enemy of the best, that you were terrorized by the tyranny of urgency, and that you enjoyed very little creative freedom.

I suggest that you start a cycle of growth and progression: a weekly cycle centered on creative activities such as reflection, planning, commitment, preparation, prevention, and relationship enhancement.

By working with my son, Joshua, in his role as quarterback of his high-school football team, I learned once again how important it is to have a creative orientation, as opposed to a problem-solving orientation. When you are problem solving, you are trying to get rid of something. When you are in a creative mode, you are trying to bring something into being. You still have to solve problems, but you solve them with a different frame of mind, a different perspective, a larger context.

I told my son, "If you create the victory in your mind before the game, then focus your proactive energies around making that happen and stop worrying about a problem you may have, you are then in a better position to create a positive outcome." As evidenced by his performance on the field, I think he learned that lesson. For example, if the weather was bad on game day, he learned to find ways to use the weather to his advantage. In effect, he learned to carry his own weather with him into the game and cause good things to happen, eventually leading his team to the state championship.

As you look back on your life, you may realize that the things that mattered most were at the mercy of things that mattered least, that the good was the enemy of the best, that you were terrorized by the tyranny of urgency, and that you enjoyed very little creative freedom.

And the net result: You frittered away much of your time, traded your life mission for minutiae, seldom exercised your unique talents and gifts, and finished precious little of the creative work you dreamed of doing.

Why Do We Focus on Problems?

Why then do we educate people, especially in schools of management, in problem-solving paradigms but not creativity? I think that is one of the great flaws in our management-education programs—the emphasis on getting rid of a problem. But we perpetuate it because creativity is harder to measure. It opens up Pandora's box. It's seen as something outside the scope of serious academic programs.

So if we aren't educated in the creative orientation, how can we acquire it—or rediscover it from our childhood? I think we have to exercise our creative imaginations. Einstein said imagination is greater than knowledge. He claimed that his remarkable scientific insights came through the power of his imagination.

The common thread in the best thinking on management and leadership is this: *People both want and need to feel that their lives and work have meaning.* For instance, if you are having difficulty in a relationship, instead of trying to solve the problem, meet with the person and come up with a common vision or purpose you can work on together. Look at what Gandhi did. He struggled with feelings of inferiority all his life, he was socially reticent, and he was fearful. But as soon as he got a sense of mission and vision about what he could do to overcome injustice, all of his weaknesses were subordinated and he dedicated his strengths to the service of his higher purpose. He became a tremendously creative person with enormous authority, power, and influence, even though he never held an official position.

> *People both want and need to buy in to transcendent purposes that give their lives and work more meaning.*

One-time Disney CEO Michael Eisner said that the main reason many companies don't progress is that they don't know how to manage people who have a creative orientation and who work with imagination. I think that it's because they define management as control, and you cannot control the creative mind. What you do is invite people to buy in to a common vision and purpose, then let them manage themselves.

Jack Welch, the legendary CEO of General Electric, used to say that his main job was to unleash the creative energy of people. It took him a long time, and some tough experiences, to learn that lesson.

Whenever I get into a problem-solving mentality, I start worrying. I start feeling anxious and stressed. I start thinking in analytical terms. In this mindset, my most important goals shrink from sight. To my dismay, the problem rarely goes away. But when I have a creative orientation and a strong sense of purpose shared with others who are most important to me, I find that problems seem to take care of themselves.

Application & Suggestions

› What is the burning *yes* that governs your life right now? It might be a vital project, a relationship that needs attention, or a personal goal. What do you need to say no to in order to realize that priority? Write down how you will say no, then do it.

› We can't deal with people as if we're dealing with things. Write in your journal: Have you been treated as a thing? How did that make you feel? How would you describe that relationship? When have you treated others as things instead of people? How did it affect the relationship?

› Important but not urgent activities are easily pushed out by daily planning, because the day is a very short horizon for substantive work. By contrast, weekly planning affords you a longer-term perspective, making it easier to act within the context of your mission, roles, and goals. If you haven't started planning your weeks, set aside time at the beginning of next week to plan how will you take care of your most important priorities and put everything else in its proper perspective.

CHAPTER 9

THE LEVER OF SACRIFICE

The first question which the priest and the Levite asked
was: "If I stop to help this man, what will happen to me?"
But . . . the good Samaritan reversed the question: "If I do
not stop to help this man, what will happen to him?"

—MARTIN LUTHER KING, JR.

Primary greatness depends on synergy—the miracle that happens
when everyone contributes their best thinking and nobody cares
about getting credit. Primary greatness depends on the principle
that we are better together than alone, that no one person can do it

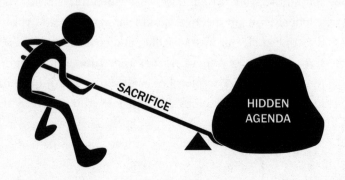

all, and that no one ever made a worthwhile contribution all alone. Burdened by "hidden agendas," too many of us are unwilling to sacrifice a little pride or ambition to serve the good of the whole. Yet, it is a much easier way to go, and ultimately more profitable for everyone.

I've learned that unless there is desire for sacrifice in our hearts, the bonding between human beings—between teacher and student, between supplier and customer, between parent and child—never happens. I've got to sacrifice my ego and willingly say, "I will be open and listen to you and see what we can create together for our mutual benefit." That involves some personal sacrifice.

To sacrifice means to revere. You can't bond with an entity—a family, a team, a company—you can only bond with *people*. That bonding occurs when a sacrifice reveres what otherwise might be disregarded. As we treat one another with more love, kindness, courtesy, humility, patience, and forgiveness, we encourage the same in return. For example, a vice president once travelled on assignment to Egypt with the president of the organization. After a particularly weary and dusty day together, he awakened the next morning to find the president quietly shining his shoes, a task the president had hoped to complete unseen.

Such quiet service in the daily and ordinary things bonds souls and awakens reciprocity in relationships. Can you imagine that vice president refusing to do anything the president asked of him on that assignment? A successful manager is one who has loved, sacrificed, served, cared for, taught, and ministered well to the needs of people.

It is the sacrifice that bonds people like nothing else. If I subordinate my ego to attend to your needs, then you begin to feel, "Well, I'll subordinate *my* ego to attend to *your* needs." Then we will ask, "What can we do to serve and help *each other*?"

To me, sacrifice is the very essence of the bonding in marriage and family relationships. For example, when I arrived home one night, I learned that my daughter Jenny was under tremendous pressure with all her papers and final tests and, on top of all that, she was putting on a party. My wife, Sandra, stayed up until two in the morning to help Jenny. That's why our children are so close to Sandra. She gives most of her evenings to them. She will sacrifice her sleep, staying up for them, then dragging herself out of bed in the morning to serve them and attend to their needs. The kids know they can rely on her.

The same principle applies to any relationship, even in business. Partnering is a key to primary greatness. Unless we are willing to work together, to sacrifice our pride of ownership of our ideas or our image, we will not meet the ever-growing demands of the marketplace.

The old levels of service will not meet future demands. It's going to take a new level of empowerment, which will come through partnering.

> › We need to partner up and down the channels with suppliers, distributors, and customers; we need strong partnerships with all stakeholders.
> › We need to partner with firms across functions. This is rarely done because of powerful misaligned structures and systems that foster internal competition and comparison.
> › We need to partner across lines of business. We gain synergy when we communicate across lines of business, not just across functions.

We need to partner with current and potential competitors to raise professional standards in our industries and to boost public perception. The multiple-listing services in real estate and the reservation system in the airline industry are classic examples of competitors working together to take care of customers. Other professionals must learn how to cooperate. If they don't enlarge the size of the pie, not just bite into each other's piece of the pie, everyone will lose.

Such partnering requires a new mindset and skillset to move toward interdependency. Few people have ever been trained in interdependency. Almost all training is focused on making us independent of each other. However, trying to get people with independent mindsets and skillsets to do interdependent partnering is like trying to play golf with a tennis racket, or tennis with a golf club.

The Case of South Africa

I have visited South Africa many times in my life. In the past, this nation underwent deep divisions. Decades ago, the economy was closed, dominated by monopolies and oligarchies that never had to deal with the demands of a global economy. In a closed economy, apartheid and white-superiority paradigms left people with few options as to how to lead their lives. But now, with an open economy and a new constitution and government, everyone has been asked to make sacrifices. That process has been going on ever since the transition happened in 1990s, and the end of the story is still unclear.

At that historic transition point, Prime Minister F. W. de Klerk came to a crisis in his own life, at which point he had to decide what the future would be for him, from both a pragmatic and a moral point of view. De Klerk was first of all a pragmatist. He could see that he needed to give up power and move toward a constitution that preserved human rights for all people. He also came to accept that position from a moral point of view, as he listened to his conscience.

Still, it took the catalyst of the late Nelson Mandela, who sacrificed twenty-seven years of his life in prison, to make that dramatic shift happen. Mandela was humbled so deeply that he came out of prison totally renewed with the spirit of reconciliation, wisdom, and moderation. During his many years in prison, he gradually reached the point at which he no longer despised his jailers. In fact, when he was elected president of South Africa, Mandela invited them to his inauguration. He was principle-centered. He knew that he had to take a responsible, moderate course, walking the fine line between the inordinately high hopes and expectations of an oppressed people and the fears and anxieties of those who had been oppressors. For his part, de Klerk overcame years of distrust and prejudice to take Mandela's hand in public and, together, they created the innovative new South Africa that strives to represent all of its people equally.

Mandela and de Klerk gave us models of self-sacrificing leadership. If they could do it in South Africa, think what you could do in your organization!

No Hidden Agendas

Anytime you reach the point at which you throw your lot into a team—or any cooperative, interdependent effort—you are at risk, and vulnerable. You take a leap of faith, and have to start being more open and honest in your communication *with no hidden agendas.*

For many people, this means sacrificing a lot. If they've been injured, it's easy to hold on to old injuries. In a politicized organization, they tend not to be open, and become duplicitous or manipulative. They talk about others behind their backs.

The manipulative style has become so prevalent that ridding themselves of that toxic behavior is a real sacrifice for many people. Without personal sacrifice, you tend to get transactional associations instead of transformational partnerships. What I've said about South Africa as a country applies to any company or person, to some extent. You won't be transformed without sacrifice. Personal sacrifice makes the difference between transaction and transformation.

The best leaders sacrifice their pride for their people and organizations. To be effective working in and with teams, we need to sacrifice our pride and seek humility. That's the nature of the sacrifice required of many professionals today—the sacrifice of ego. We need to enter into our relationships with each other in a spirit of mutual respect.

When Benjamin Franklin was trying to cultivate humility, he "made it a rule" not to be abrupt with people but to show respect for their opinions. He was also careful not to be too "dogmatic" in his own opinions. As an elderly man, he wrote, "For these fifty years past no one has ever heard a dogmatic expression escape me." As a result, he reported that he grew in his influence with others.[10] A dogmatic statement might be, "I'm right, and anyone who disagrees with me is wrong."

The key to transformational partnerships is the willingness to sacrifice an old mindset and skillset and to move to the new mindset of interdependency and the new skillset of synergy, seeking first to understand while always looking for mutual benefit.

> *Anytime you reach the point at which you throw your lot into a team—or any cooperative, interdependent effort—you are at risk, and vulnerable. You take a leap of faith, and have to start being more open and honest in your communication with no hidden agendas.*

People need to be emotionally secure to arrive at a common vision. Everyone who works on a jigsaw puzzle must have the same final picture in mind. In most organizations, there isn't a final picture in mind; people see different pictures. And since everyone has to act anyway, they act on misinformation, wrong information, or no information. They may complete a section of the puzzle, but they can't fit it with other sections.

Sacrificing for the Team

All team members need to sacrifice their own incomplete paradigms and learn to align with true-north principles. Sacrificing a cherished mindset is often the hardest sacrifice of all. It takes humility because the traditional mindset is "I'm here to serve my own interests. I'm going to control the agenda." This mindset leads to arrogance—the sort of pride that comes before the fall. Humility says, "I am not in control; principles ultimately govern and control."

The team has to know and use high-leverage principles in their work together.

They must be men and women of integrity who cultivate an abundance mindset. With abundance thinking, they won't be constantly competing and comparing themselves with each other or feel the need to play political games, because their security comes from within.

They must be willing to challenge all paradigms. It takes tremendous courage and deep introspection to throw off habitual ways of thinking, which they must do if those habits aren't productive. When we confront our own thinking, we experience the fear of replacing an old habit with something new. Most people operate comfortably within their existing paradigms, but the teams of today must have the courage to surface those paradigms, identify the underlying assumptions and motivations, and challenge them by asking, "Does this still hold water?"

They must seek "win-win or no deal" options. Synergy is more than cooperation; it's creating better solutions. It requires Empathic Listening and courage in expressing views and opinions. Out of genuine interaction comes synergy.

They must be trustworthy. No one can be trusted who is not in alignment with true principles. Becoming principle-centered gives us the character strength to give up our grasping for power and control and stop treating people as a means to an end.

New Sources of Power

Today's team leaders must look to new sources of power. The sources of their power are shifting: from position to persuasion, from charm to character, from control to service and sacrifice, from pride to humility, and from credentials to continuous learning and improvement. Their power must come from four character-based sources.

THE WISE EXERCISE OF SELF-AWARENESS, IMAGINATION, INDEPENDENT WILL, AND CONSCIENCE. Unless people exercise these four endowments responsibly, their team efforts will eventually fizzle. Team leaders must challenge any paradigm that ignores the responsible use of these freedoms.

SPENDING MORE TIME DOING THINGS THAT ARE IMPORTANT BUT NOT NECESSARILY URGENT. As noted earlier, when we surveyed Deming Award–winning companies, we found that their executives spend 60 percent of their time doing things that are important but not urgent (things such as creating vision, mission, direction, and recreation).

CONTINUOUS LEARNING, IMPROVING, AND PROGRESSING. Team leaders regularly assess results, receive feedback, and make necessary corrections and improvements.

HAVING A NETWORK OF WIN-WIN RELATIONSHIPS AND PARTNER-SHIPS. Through personal humility and sacrifice, we naturally improve our relationships and establish strong partnerships. All our relationships take on the spirit of teaming, partnering, synergistic cooperation, and interdependency.

There is no sacrifice without humility. Either we are forced by circumstance to be humble, or we can choose to be humble in the realization that principles ultimately govern. To be humble is good, regardless of the reason. But it's better to be humbled by conscience than by circumstance.

Application & Suggestions

> To be effective working in and with teams, we need to sacrifice our pride and seek humility. In what way is your personal ego a barrier to team progress? Resolve to take down that barrier. What happens when you do?

> Most people operate within existing paradigms. What paradigms do you or your team or your family have that might be working against you? Have the courage to bring those paradigms to the surface, identify the underlying assumptions and motivations, and challenge them by asking, "Does this still hold water?" Which paradigms do you need to sacrifice to get better results? Record the results in your journal.

> Explain to someone else the concept of synergy, then have that person explain it to you. What did you learn from that exercise?

> The main motivator of personal change is pain. If you're in pain, you are more open to humility and personal sacrifice, leading to inside-out, principle-centered change. Where does your life or profession give you pain? What is the source of it? Write down steps you can take to bring your life more in alignment with principles of effectiveness and lessen the pain.

CHAPTER 10

THE LEVER OF SERVICE

At the end of life, we will not be judged by how many diplomas
we have received, how much money we have made, how
many great things we have done. We will be judged by "I was
hungry, and you gave me something to eat, I was naked and
you clothed me. I was homeless, and you took me in."

—MOTHER TERESA

With people, the little things are the big things. The principle of service is highly personal—it's a giving of the self. The personal touch matters with 90 percent of people, and it empowers the rest. Self-

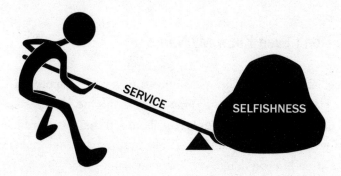

ishness is the source of our heaviest burdens in life, while serving others—lightening the burdens of others—is the very essence of primary greatness. Secondary greatness has nothing to do with service.

A friend of mine, an actor, was once in a theater in New York City watching a friend of his, a fellow actor, up on stage. My friend could see that his colleague wasn't connecting with the audience, and so he worked his way into the orchestra pit with the intent of giving his friend a message.

Knowing the play very well, the man knew exactly where his friend would be on the stage at different times. He knew that in one scene his friend would stand just one foot away from the orchestra pit, and he hoped to deliver his message in that brief window of opportunity.

So when his friend stood on that spot, he raised his head up, caught the eye of his friend, and said three words: "Talk to me."

His friend instantly got the message—that he was talking to a glazed-over audience that he couldn't see at all—it was just a great amorphous mass out there. When his friend said, "Talk to me," he knew that meant to deal with the person, a real individual with feelings and perceptions, someone who matters. Instantly, he began acting to individuals, even though he couldn't see most of them because of the strong stage lights. But he could see some faces, and he essentially talked to the one. Soon he captured the audience right back. He connected, because the key to the many is the one.

You Don't Even Know My Name

Once, when I was teaching at a university, a student approached me after class at the end of the semester to thank me for the content I had delivered. It was a huge class of about 550 students. He added, "I admire what you've done in this field, and respect your knowledge, Mr. Covey, but you don't even know my name."

That confirmed to me the old truth: "I don't care how much you know until I know how much you care."

Recently, I was teaching a large group and going through a series of slides. I asked the technical assistant, "Now let's see this slide; now let's see the next slide." I later received a letter from one of the audience members who said, "I listened all afternoon. Not once did you say please or thank you."

I thought that I was kindly in my voice. I didn't bark out orders; nevertheless, I failed to say the magic words, and the message to that person was not the content—it was a feeling that I lacked common courtesy and respect.

Such feedback suggests that the personal touch matters with 90 percent of people, and it empowers the rest.

A friend who is a prominent professional athlete teaches a class of four-year-old children in his church during the off-season. He loves those kids. He knows them by name and he calls them by name. He affirms their value and worth. He takes a special interest in them and takes time to greet them. As a result, they wouldn't miss his class for anything. They want to climb all over him and sit on his lap. He focuses on the one, as each child is important to him.

Our customers are no different from these children. They want to be called by name. They want to feel that the company representative really cares about them. That makes a huge difference; in fact, it's often the deal maker or breaker. With people, the little things are the big things.

Why Serving the One Works

Why is this principle—the key to the many is the one—so important? Why does it open hearts and minds and doors? I think it's because the deepest hunger of the human soul is to be recognized, valued, appreciated, and understood. When you acknowledge the presence of others, and adapt your presentation in an effort to reach them, in effect you say to them, "You matter. You're a person of worth. You have intrinsic merit, and I'm not comparing you with anyone. You are precious. And if you allow me into your mind to leave a message, I know that I'm on sacred ground." I think that's what it means.

> *The deepest hunger of the human soul is to be recognized, valued, appreciated, and understood.*

As a customer, I can usually tell if frontline service providers are totally present during the few seconds we interact, as they take my order or deal with my request. If they're totally present, I sense that they really care.

Caring about the individual works because it's a paradigm focused on people, not things; it's focused on relationships, not schedules; it's focused on effectiveness, not efficiency; it's focused on personal leadership, not resource management.

What a difference it makes to work in a caring culture. For instance, my daughter Jenny started a job in the customer-service area of our company. At the end of her six-week training period, she said to me, "Dad, I feel sad to come to the end of this training." I said, "Why?" She said, "I will miss the other team members so much." I said, "Why?" She said, "We are a team. If there's ever a mistake, it's a team mistake, and everyone comes to support. Our team leaders are servant leaders, not bosses. And their care for us models how we should care for our customers."

She continued, "Even though I'm only on the phone and never meet any of these people, I've cultivated relationships with many customers who call me back as a friend, who write me letters. Some of them I've only talked with once and yet when they call in to make an order, they ask me what I would recommend." She learned that there is a direct correlation between how she is treated as a member of the service team and how she treats customers, and how they treat her.

Three Ways to Get It

So how do you get this concern for the individual customer? I see three ways: hire it, train it, or cultivate it in the culture.

HIRE IT. When evaluating prospective employees, a major airline brings candidates into a room, and asks each person to make a presentation. Everyone thinks company officials are evaluating the person making the presentation. But they're really evaluating, through hidden video cameras, the people in the audience who are watching the presentations. If they are attentive, supportive, and seem to care, they know they're getting someone who naturally has that ability or disposition to care about others. If someone is totally self-absorbed or bored before or after making his or her presentation, having no sense of rapport with the person who's up there struggling, then that's a strong negative signal.

TRAIN IT. In another organization, executives want to identify those employees who are naturally team players. They do this by giving each team a particular task with a tight deadline. The task is of sufficient complexity and difficulty that the expertise of other people is needed. They have to work as a team to get it done. What they find is that natural tendencies and inclinations surface rapidly. Those who are not team players immediately try to take control. They ignore some people, they put down others, they are discourteous, but they are very task-oriented. Others are very relationship-oriented, but they have no sense of the task. They never accomplish anything.

Now, the big surprise is that the evaluators of each person's team skills are the other members of the team. People are aghast when they discover this at the end and realize, "My gosh, look how I treated those people."

CULTIVATE IT. You might hire it and train it, but to me the most powerful way to cultivate the service ethic is to develop strong social norms in the culture itself. When people begin to see that this is how we treat each other, you will then have a sustainable competitive advantage.

The cultivation of the spirit of servant leadership will teach everyone to be kind, respectful, and caring, even though some people aren't naturally that way.

I once visited with the director of human resources of The Ritz-Carlton. Their company motto is "Ladies and gentlemen serving ladies and gentlemen." I asked this woman, "Has this motto, this culture of respect, influenced your personal and your family life?"

She said to me, "Absolutely. It's like night and day. I was raised in a very difficult situation. I was abused and battered as a foster child. I went back and forth between different homes and situations. And I developed a survival mindset. I was angry and cynical on the inside, but used human-relations techniques on the surface in an effort to be nice to people in the company and the customers. But once off work, if someone rubbed me wrong, I took my frustrations out on them."

I reminded her, "Unexpressed feelings never die—they're just buried alive and come forth later in uglier ways."

She said, "Mine came forth constantly on my loved ones . . . until I started working here."

I asked, "How is it different?"

She said, "Being in this company is almost like having a second family and childhood. People in this organization are models to me. Now I see and treat my children differently. I'm more interested in creating a wonderful feeling and atmosphere at home than I am in getting a particular job done."

A man from the same organization, but a different hotel, said essentially the same thing. He said, "You know, this is such an attractive culture to me—it's been such a family to me—that when I go on vacation, I prefer to stay in the lobby and watch the hotel employees interact with customers. I just love the niceness with which people treat each other."

So much of this civility and courtesy has eroded to cynicism and manipulation in our society. Even at the more exclusive hotels and resorts, I don't think you can expect genuine civility. Money can't guarantee it. In fact, wealth might foster an elitist attitude among service providers who merely manipulate guests with human-relations skills for the sake of getting tips.

On a recent flight, I observed a pregnant woman as she entered the plane carrying a child in one arm and a large bag in the other. Two flight attendants stood nearby, talking to each other, as this woman came through. I stood up and said, "Let me help you." The flight attendants continued to watch as we struggled to get stuff into the storage bin. Maybe it's not part of their job description, but if it's their job spirit, they will help. I suspect that's the same way they are treated inside the company—their complaints are ignored.

I took my son to get onto the ski lift for his very first time. He was just terrified of the ski lift. I had to encourage him to try and told him, "Don't worry, I'll ask them to slow it down."

As we approached the lift, I asked the operator, "Could you please slow it down? This is his first time."

He frowned—in fact, he looked disgusted—and said, "Well, okay."

From that moment on, my son lost interest in skiing.

When you're vulnerable, you can be hurt by the slightest inclination or nuance in someone's voice. Kids have a sixth sense for that stuff. Often they're damaged by the cynicism of others. They pick up those vibes instantly. So, that was the end of his skiing career.

My guess is that the lift operator received the same treatment when he went to his supervisor and said, "Can I get this day off to attend a family reunion?" His supervisor probably snapped and said, "Who do you think you are? You're scheduled to work here that day."

And then that supervisor probably got treated the same way by an arbitrary and capricious boss.

The older I get, the more clearly I see the connection between the way employees are treated and how they treat customers. It's a chain reaction.

Of course, we need not run around like reactive beings. We can learn not to be offended. We can cultivate our security from within, based on integrity to fundamental principles, so that we can love when we're not loved, be kind when people aren't kind to us, and be patient when others are impatient with us.

> *The older I get, the more clearly I see the connection between the way employees are treated and how they treat customers. It's like a chain reaction.*

The capacity to turn the other cheek, go the extra mile, and be a servant leader comes from a deep vision of what we're trying to accomplish. We see what we seek. If we seek a great thing, we tend to see greatness in other people. And we seek feedback from people who have the courage to share. We're not killing the messenger who brings us feedback. Rather, we show appreciation and have the humility to apologize and say, "I need to improve and make amends." Such behavior gives you the ability to want to be more civil to the next person.

Application & Suggestions

› "You matter. You're a person of worth. You have intrinsic merit, and I'm not comparing you with anyone. You are precious. And if you allow me into your mind to leave a message, I know that I'm on sacred ground." Have you experienced this level of relationship with anyone? With whom can you cultivate this type of relationship? Write down one or two steps you will take to build that relationship.

> There is a connection between the way employees are treated and how they treat customers. It's a chain reaction. What is happening along your chain? Where is the chain weak or in trouble? What can you do today to strengthen the connection between yourself and a colleague?

> We must learn not to be offended, to refuse to self-alienate. How? We can cultivate our security from within, based on integrity to fundamental principles, so that we can love when we're not loved, be kind when people aren't kind to us, and be patient when others are impatient with us. The next time you feel offended or slighted, try patience. What difference does it make to your attitude?

CHAPTER 11

THE LEVER OF RESPONSIBILITY

The final forming of a person's character lies in their own hands.

—ANNE FRANK

Taking responsibility is essential to primary greatness. It's easy to take responsibility for the good things in our lives, but the real test comes when things aren't going well. Those who shrug off responsibility for their lives, blaming circumstances or other people for their situation, become professional victims. Those who practice primary greatness know that their quality of life depends on their own choices, not on the choices of others or even their circumstances.

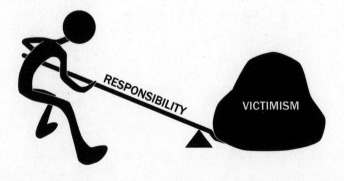

An executive once told me: "My biggest worry and concern is my poor relationship with my most creative people at work and with my teenage son at home. In the past, I have lost my temper and yelled at them. How can I improve these relationships and change the image they have of me?"

Fortunately, no situation is hopeless. There are several powerful ways to heal a broken relationship, to restore the Emotional Bank Account, and to have a positive influence again.

The Uttermost Farthing

People often are offended—or they offend others—and then neither party has the humility to take full responsibility for their part. Instead, they rationalize and justify themselves. They look for evidence to support their perception of the other person, which only aggravates the original problem. Ultimately, they put each other into a mental-emotional prison.

You can't come out of that prison until you pay the uttermost farthing. A farthing was a tiny English coin equaling one fourth of a penny. Paying the uttermost farthing means paying the price that's required. It means a humble and complete acknowledgment of your responsibility for the problem, even though others might be partly responsible as well. If you take full responsibility for your part in it—and acknowledge it and apologize out of deep sincerity and concession of spirit—the other person will sense the utter sincerity of what you say. Of course, your behavior must then comport with that expression, so that others can see your integrity.

Paying the uttermost farthing requires behavior consistent with the apology over a period of time, because your Emotional Bank Account with that person may be so overdrawn that no apology will redeem it. You might have to do much more. You have to show your sincerity. You can't talk yourself out of problems you behave yourself into—particularly if you're constantly apologizing but your behavior pattern and style remain unchanged.

If you pay only the first farthing, expecting other people to also acknowledge their part and their responsibility, that is insufficient. The other person may pay one farthing with the attitude, "Well, I'm sorry, but it's not all one way. You've been a party to this thing as well." But he won't pay a second farthing until you pay the uttermost farthing.

To pay the uttermost farthing, you might say, "I was wrong." "I embarrassed you in front of your friends." Or "I cut you off in that meeting, when you had made this tremendous preparation. And I'm not only going to apologize to you, but also to the other people who were in that meeting, because they could see the way I dealt with you, and it offended them as well." You make no effort to justify, explain, defend, or blame in any way—you make every effort to pay the uttermost farthing in order to get out of prison.

What happens when you pay the full price? Assume, to begin with, that relationships are strained and that you are at least partly responsible. If you merely try to be better and not confess and apologize, the other person will still be suspicious of you. He has been hurt and wounded; therefore, his guard is up. He will question your new behavior, your kind face, and wonder what might happen next. Your improved behavior and manner won't assuage his distrust. Nothing you can do will change it, because you are behind bars and walls in a prison of his own making in his mind. The bars and walls are the mental and emotional labels he has put upon you. Only by making a complete and specific acknowledgment of your own failings or mistakes do you pay the uttermost farthing.

The Principle in Practice

I constantly rediscover the efficacy of this age-old principle in my work with people who are low in desire and responsibility and who tend to blame others for their poor performance.

I once worked with a young man who was barely getting along in the organization I was leading. I labeled him as an underachiever and, for months, every time I saw his face or heard his name, I would think of him in this way.

I became aware of how I had labeled him and how this label had become a self-fulfilling prophecy. I realized that people tend to become like you treat them or be-lieve them to be. I decided that I needed to pay the uttermost farthing. I went to

> People tend to become like you treat them or believe them to be.

this young man, confessed what I believed had happened and how I had played a role, and asked for his forgiveness.

Our relationship began on a new base of honesty. Eventually, he grew in his role and performed magnificently.

The theme of many novels is unrequited love, when people simply refuse to love unconditionally because they've been wounded and hurt before. And so they recoil and defend themselves by withdrawing inside themselves and being cynical, suspicious, or sarcastic. They're not open because they don't want to be vulnerable.

I once told my daughter after she had been hurt in a relationship, "Be sure you maintain your vulnerability." She said, "Why? It hurts too much." And I said, "Well, you don't need to get your security from that relationship. If you get your security from your integrity, you can still maintain your vulnerability. That's what makes you beautiful and lovely—your willingness to be open and authentic. If you reject other people and new opportunities because you've been rejected, you will build a shell around yourself that will keep you from being loved. One of the lovely things about you is your willingness to trust and to risk being hurt."

Clearing the Legal Hurdle

Many people face a legal barrier to paying the uttermost farthing. For example, some lawyers might caution their clients against making any form of apology in order to maintain 100 percent innocence, because apologizing might imply guilt.

Many business leaders have their own thinking straitjacketed by legalities and by an attorney's mindset. While protection is prudent in some cases, thinking like a lawyer can contribute to future problems. It's like drafting a premarital contract: "In the event we have a divorce, this is how we'll settle the estate." Such contracts may actually contribute to a breakup. They may be realistic, but they're not idealistic. And if we abandon our ideals, we abandon the essence of our humanity—our ability to rise above tendencies of self-protectiveness and defensiveness.

As we develop a legal mindset, we imagine worst-case scenarios, assume the worst of other people, and seek evidence to justify our position. Such thinking becomes a causal, contributing force of adversarialism. We need to work with attorneys who have the ability to transcend the legal mindset, who know when and how to properly apply their skills but who have a more positive attitude toward life and people.

Many problems can be resolved in business if only someone will admit up front, "I was wrong." For example, I met with a chief executive officer who said that the union leaders had walked out of an important meeting with him earlier that day. I asked, "Why?" He admitted that the company had mistreated some union member, but that it was a "very minor issue."

I said, "Well, to that union, their mission is your minutiae. And you've got to apologize. If you're wrong, you've got to acknowledge it, right now, today. Don't go another hour. Call them at once, while you are still on speaking terms."

The chief executive did as I suggested, and his sincere apology was well received by the union leaders; in fact, it caused them to come back to the meeting. A simple apology can have that kind of leverage with people.

I'm convinced that this principle will work wonders to resolve differences, heal relationships, settle strikes, and foster international business deals. When a relationship is formed between people on a very personal level, the spirit of paying the uttermost farthing is stirred up. People say, "I was wrong. I apologize, and I want to make it up to you."

Paying the uttermost farthing also means making the effort to get to know the other person better. In ancient Greek, *enemy* and *stranger* were the same word—*xenos*. By getting to know our enemies on a very personal level, they will cease being strangers. Little by little, we create a culture of civility and service where members know that each person has weaknesses, but they have the humility, authenticity, and honesty to confess them and to try to compensate for them.

Six Points

When applying this principle to any seriously broken or strained relationship, I emphasize six points.

WE MAY HONESTLY ADMIT TO OURSELVES THAT WE ARE AT LEAST PARTLY TO BLAME FOR THE PROBLEM. Upon reflection, we can see how we hurt, insulted, or belittled another, or how we failed to understand, or how we were inconsistent in discipline or conditional in love.

Often what happens when leaders fail to pay the uttermost far-thing is that they lose their moral authority. Moral authority makes up much of the power we have as leaders, especially in flattened organizations in which there are many knowledge workers. In an information world, you can't throw your weight around, because the same information is available to everyone. Your moral authority is the most powerful thing you've got.

WHEN PEOPLE ARE DEEPLY HURT OR EMBARRASSED, THEY DRAW BACK AND CLOSE UP. They go into a victim mentality. They refuse to release us from the mental prison they have put us in. To avoid future hurt, they judge us as unkind, unfair, or not understanding.

IMPROVING OUR BEHAVIOR ALONE WON'T RELEASE US FROM THIS PRISON, SIMPLY BECAUSE THEY CAN'T AFFORD TO TRUST US AGAIN. It's too risky. They are suspicious of this new behavior, this new face, this insincere entreaty. They might say, "I trusted him before and look what happened." Although inside they cry out for direction and emotional support, they keep us in a mental prison for an indeterminate sentence.

OFTEN THE ONLY WAY OUT IS TO GO TO THEM AND ADMIT OUR MISTAKES, APOLOGIZE, AND ASK FORGIVENESS. In this reconciliation, we must be specific in describing what we did that was wrong. We make no excuses, explanations, or defenses. We simply acknowledge that we know we did wrong, we understand what put us in prison, and we want to pay the price of release. If we only make a stab at this process, but inwardly hold back by saying, "He should be sorry too; I can only go so far, but no further until he acknowledges his part," then our peacemaking is superficial, insincere, and manipulative. Under the surface, the suspicion and turbulence still rage, as the next stress on the relationship will reveal.

THIS APPROACH MUST BE UTTERLY SINCERE AND NOT USED AS A MANIPULATIVE TECHNIQUE TO BRING OTHERS AROUND. If this approach is used only because it works, it will boomerang. Above all, we must not see ourselves as victims too. Unless sincere change takes place deep within us, sooner or later we'll trespass again on tender feelings, and the new mental prison will have thicker walls than ever. Others simply will not believe us when we say again how sorry we are. Repeated token apologies win no confidence or forgiveness.

IN MOST SITUATIONS, PAYING THE UTTERMOST FARTHING WORKS NOT ONLY TO OBTAIN A RELEASE FROM PRISON, WITH ITS NEW OPPORTUNITY TO COMMUNICATE AND TO INFLUENCE, BUT ALSO TO INSPIRE, NOT FORCE, OTHERS TO MAKE SOME HARD ADMISSIONS AND RESOLVES TOO. Sometimes, in our hearts, we know we have crossed the sensitive line and hurt, insulted, or offended other people. We may have felt justified at the time, as they may have deserved this treatment, but we learn that when we hurt others, we need to go to them, acknowledge it, and seek their forgiveness. Pride often keeps us from paying the uttermost farthing, but eventually we must swallow our pride, express our sorrow, apologize, and seek forgiveness.

Application & Suggestions

> › Has anyone sincerely and humbly asked for your forgiveness? How did that affect your relationship? Who needs an apology from you? Try it. How did it go? How did it affect the relationship?
> › Do you feel anger or resentment toward certain people? Do you feel like a victim? What will be the consequences of those feelings over time? What can you do today to start ridding yourself of those feelings?

> Do you find yourself constantly apologizing while your behavior continues unchanged? What will be the consequences over time? What one thing can you change about yourself that is keeping you from building better relationships with others?

CHAPTER 12

THE LEVER OF LOYALTY

Great minds discuss ideas. Average minds discuss
events. Small minds discuss people.

—ELEANOR ROOSEVELT

People with primary greatness are loyal; not unquestioningly loyal,
but they show the kind of loyalty that refuses to stereotype, castigate,
or label others in their absence. Too many of us carry the burden of
disrespect for others, of conceit or even contempt for the imperfec-
tions of the people around us. We unload a tremendous weight from

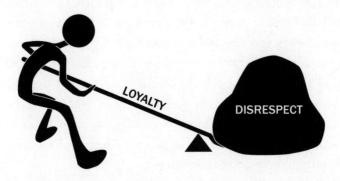

ourselves if we can cast off unrealistic expectations of others and stay loyal to them as human beings.

The ultimate test of primary greatness is to be loyal to people who are absent.

When other people are not with you, they're in the dark; they don't know what you're saying about them or whether you're loyal to them. And that's when you show your true character. That doesn't mean you can't be critical, but you're constructively critical and loyal to the point that you would not be ashamed if they happened to overhear the conversation, or if word were to get back to them, as it often does. You don't just sit on the sideline cutting, labeling, and stereotyping people and then look for evidence to support your disdain for them.

Four Short Stories

Perhaps a few stories will help make this point.

I was once a faculty member at a university in Hawaii. I was very upset about our housing situation, so I went directly to the president, since he worked with me on my visiting professorship. In the meeting, I complained about his housing director, who seemed to me to be incompetent and uncaring.

The president immediately said to me, "Stephen, I'm sorry to hear about your housing situation. But I want you to know that our housing director is a very fine and competent person. Why don't we have him come here right now so we can solve the problem together?"

Can you see how loyal the president was toward that man? I was embarrassed, because the president was so right in what he was doing. I hesitated to say to him, "No, you go ahead and handle it. I just wanted you to be aware of the problem," because he was forcing me to take the responsible position too.

Well, the president got on the phone and invited this man to join us. Soon I could see this guy walking across the campus. Meanwhile, I was thinking, "I wonder if I communicated clearly? Maybe I'm partly responsible for this mess." By the time the housing director arrived, I was very mellow and humble.

I was also very impressed by the character of this president, by his loyalty to the absent director, even though it was embarrassing to me. The president was teaching me a correct principle the hard way.

> *When other people are not with you, they're in the dark—they don't know what's happening, what you're saying about them, and whether you are loyal to them. And that's when you show your true character.*

When the housing director entered the room, my whole attitude had changed. I was nice to the guy: "How are you? Nice to see you." Just minutes before, I was criticizing the guy behind his back. The president could sense my duplicity, which added to my embarrassment.

But this was a powerful learning experience for me. I learned not to talk behind people's backs in ways that I would be ashamed to have them overhear. People who are present know that you will do the same thing to them, especially if there is a strain on your relationship.

One time I told the story about the housing director in a speech I was giving. After my speech, a senior executive of a large bank came up to me and said, "I've had a similar experience. I visited one of our branch banks and was served by one of the tellers. The service was so poor that I complained to the department head about the woman who served me. Most department heads are so awed by my very presence that they can hardly even deal with me. But this department head said, 'I'm sorry to hear about your bad experience. She's such a fine person. Let's call her in and talk this through together. Maybe you can tell her directly what your experience was.'"

The executive then said to the department head, "No, go ahead and handle it. I just wanted you to be aware. I don't want to get involved." But the department head said to this executive, "Well, I know that if it were me, I'd want to get involved. If you were this teller, wouldn't you want to be involved?"

Imagine the courage it took for this department head to deal with the executive vice president of the bank in that direct, truthful manner. The answer was so self-evident: "Yeah, I guess I would." "Well, then, let's call her in." So she came in, and they dealt with it. The person received the feedback, and it was handled in a responsible way.

The vice president then told me, "Later, when we were trying to select a president for one of our branch banks, I nominated this department head totally on the basis of that experience, because I knew if he would have such courage, honesty, and loyalty to someone who wasn't there, even in the face of a highly positioned individual, he would handle other matters with integrity."

Once, a manager of a remote service station trained his staff how to make more profits from customers by finding nonexistent problems with their cars.

So when a car pulls in, the manager first sees the plates and says, "Notice this is an out-of-towner. That means you'll probably never see the person again, so try to learn if the person knows anything about his car. Talk to him about some technical thing under the hood. You might say, 'Your starting motor looks like it might go out on you.' If the person says, 'Starting motor? What's that?' then you know you've got a total idiot, so you can do whatever you want."

You then say, "Well, if it were my car, I wouldn't want to take a chance with my starting motor, especially driving through the desert. I could be stranded."

"I can't have that happen. What should I do?"

"Well, we could give you a good deal on a new one. I'll sell you one at cost and throw in all the labor free."

So the victim thinks, "What a deal I got! I only had to pay two hundred dollars for the starting motor. It was normally three hundred forty-nine dollars with labor."

But the manager winks at his attendants, knowing he has a 40 percent margin built into the price of the motor.

Later, the staffers huddle and say to each other, "Now, if this guy would do that to his customers, how is he going to deal with us?" They know that the manager will look for ways to cheat them as well.

I was at the Canadian border, and I went into a store where there was a half-price sale going on. I started looking at a leather coat marked 50 percent off. I was the only customer in the store, but there were two salespeople and the owner-manager. The manager said to me, "What a deal this is." He really sold me on it. The coat fit me well, and I liked it.

I then said to him, "Even with this discount, it could be expensive. How much duty would I have to pay?"

He said, "None. You don't have to pay anything on this."

I said, "Well, it says on the customs form that I must declare everything I purchase abroad."

He said, "Don't worry about it. Just wear it. Everyone else does it."

I said, "But I signed the form."

He said, "Listen, mister, everyone does it. They won't even ask you questions. Just wear the coat when you cross the border. Don't worry about it."

And I said, "Well, the thing that worries me most is what these two gentlemen behind you might think now about how you will deal with them on matters of commission, career training, and things of this nature."

The manager and the two salespeople all blushed.

So, What's the Big Deal?

Now, you might say, "Every organization has its competitors and its enemies. Why is it such a big deal to talk about them in a cavalier or casual way?"

It's a big deal because if you allow people around you to stereotype, castigate, and label others, you essentially tell them that you would make snide remarks about them behind their backs. You tell them that you're not centered on principles; you're seeking gain, pleasure, or popularity at someone else's expense. If you talk loosely about a customer, you will likely talk loosely about employees and suppliers.

> *The key to the ninety-nine is the one. If people know that you treat one person with respect then, under different circumstances, you would likely treat them the same way, even if there were some strain or pressure added.*

I think the key to the ninety-nine is the one. If people know that you treat one person with respect, then under different circumstances, you would likely treat them the same way, even if there were some small strain or pressure added.

In meetings, we often talk about people who are not in attendance in demeaning ways to undermine their position or cut their credibility in the eyes of others.

Many times I have defended people who were absent from meetings. I won't allow people around me to label and castigate those who are absent. When a glib remark is made, I'll say, "Wait a minute. That's not the way we want to talk about people." I may also point out what good that person has done. I may also be critical of the person, but I would not be ashamed to have the person there.

When you defend the integrity of a person who is absent, what does that say to those who are present? It says that you would do the same thing for them. Sure, it takes courage to speak up at the time. It's much easier to say nothing. But I believe that if we have a chance to defend others or to speak up for our cherished beliefs and values, we need to do it.

Other Ways to Be Loyal

What are some other ways to be loyal? Here are seven.

DEFEND THE DEFENSELESS—THE OUTCAST, THE UNDERDOG, THE LOW PERSON ON THE TOTEM POLE, THE MINORITY, THE SCAPEGOAT. I like what Dag Hammarskjöld, the great Secretary-General of the United Nations, said: "It is more noble to give yourself completely to one individual than to labor diligently for the salvation of the masses." When we attend to the one, it shows our character, and affects the many.

Just look what we do in a democracy to preserve the rights of the one. Even though we don't achieve perfect justice, we try to do justice—that's the ideal. We aspire to the ideal of justice.

ANTICIPATE DISCUSSION AND GET CLEARANCE. Suppose you know in advance of a meeting at which some controversial person and position will be discussed. It would be wise to call that person and say, "I know you can't be present, but would it be all right if I talk about you or represent your position in this way?"

CALL THE PERSON AFTER THE DISCUSSION AND REPORT WHAT WAS SAID. You could call the person and say, "This is what happened, and this is what was said, and here is what we did." This is very important when you think what was said might get misrepresented. You might say, "I want to be clear as to my intentions and what I said."

THINK OF THE CUSTOMERS WHO ARE NOT PRESENT. The whole quality movement focuses on the customer. Business has gradually come to realize that customers and suppliers—all stakeholders—must be treated with respect.

BRING UP THE BACKGROUND OF THE PERSON OR THE CONTEXT OF THE EVENT. With more geographic distance and cultural diversity, there's more potential for divisiveness and differences. When a person is being demeaned or talked about in a negative way, you may need to remind others: "This person is from a different culture or background, so rather than be such harsh critics, let's try to understand and give them the benefit of the doubt."

GIVE PEOPLE A CHANCE TO EXPLAIN OR DEFEND THEIR POSITION OR THE CIRCUMSTANCE IN THE NEXT MEETING. Every person wants his or her day in court—a chance to explain what happened and why.

BRING UP THE BRIGHT SIDE, THE POSITIVE SIDE OF THE PERSON. When I was meeting with members of a project team, team members started bashing a person whom they perceived to be a competitor. I said, "I don't think he would be comfortable with that judgment. I think he deserves better. He's one of the great presenters of our time."

People can often tell when others are gossiping about them. They may sense that their name is being trashed, that their enemies are conspiring against them. I think that's more common than we know. I think people have a sixth sense as to when they're being slighted.

Also, I see that many idle words spoken in secret or written without consideration are later published or broadcast. So one of the best reasons for defending people who are absent is that those idle words—those character assassinations, hasty judgments, and poor decisions—won't come back to haunt you.

Application & Suggestions

> Write your answers: When have you participated in talking about people behind their backs? What is the consequence of this behavior to your own character? to other people's view of you? When you defend the integrity of a person who is absent, what does that say to those who are present?
> The next time people within your hearing are criticizing or discussing a person who is absent, decline to participate. See what happens as a result.
> Who needs constructive feedback from you? Make a plan to provide the constructive feedback. Record the results and your feelings about the meeting.
> "It is more noble to give yourself completely to one individual than to labor diligently for the salvation of the masses." What does this mean to you? What one individual needs your dedication and devotion? Write down what you can do to give yourself more completely to that person.

CHAPTER 13

THE LEVER OF RECIPROCITY

It is an absolute human certainty that no one can know his own beauty or perceive a sense of his own worth until it has been reflected back to him in the mirror of another loving, caring human being.

—JOHN JOSEPH POWELL

Primary greatness is based on the principle of reciprocity—that what you give comes back to you. The concept of fairness is deeply ingrained in every culture. Those who believe in secondary greatness want to tip the scales of every human interaction in their favor—their

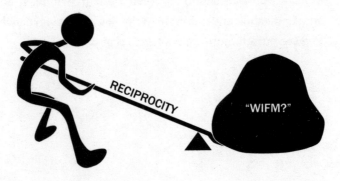

motto is "WIFM": What's in it for me? By contrast, those who live by the principle of reciprocity know there is no win in life if others do not win too.

What's in it for me? That's the only question some people ever ask. And when those people happen to be your friends, children, or spouse, you face a major challenge. As in business, if those people happen to be your employees and customers, you face a similar challenge—to change the relationship from a win-lose, one-way experience to a reciprocal, mutually rewarding relationship. Customers and suppliers will seek their own self-interest unless leaders learn how to cultivate reciprocal relationships.

In business, for example, customer service is often a one-way street. Just listen to frontline service providers: "You give and give, and they take and take without any thanks."

They say things like this: "There is not much customer loyalty any more. If there's a better price, product, or program on the market, customers will shop and switch. Even when we do our best to build strong customer relationships, many customers will go where the price is lower."

"Many times we make our customers the beneficiaries of some wonderful service program, and they take advantage of it and run."

Customers, of course, often see things the opposite way:

"They're very glad to take your money, but just try to get them to answer a question or respond to an email."

"It seems like you pay more and more and get less and less service—everywhere from the airlines to the doctor's office."

Six Steps Beyond Hit and Run

How can we ensure that the most important relationships in our lives are reciprocal?

So much depends on the nature of the relationship. If that relationship is based upon mutual understanding, then bonding starts to happen, and the relationship becomes mutually beneficial.

LOOK FIRST TO YOURSELF. To improve your relationships, don't look to others to change and don't look to easy shortcuts. Look to yourself. Be honest with yourself first: The roots of your problems are in your character, and so are the root solutions. Build your character and your relationships on the bedrock of principles.

Our relationship with ourselves affects and is influenced by relationships with others; conversely, our relationship with others is based on our relationship with ourselves. Our ability to get along well with others flows naturally from how well we get along with ourselves—from our own internal peace and harmony.

> *To improve your relationships, don't look to others to change and don't look to easy shortcuts. Look to yourself. Be honest with yourself first.*

To get closer to partners or customers, for example, we may need to make some changes in our own attitudes and behaviors. When I like and respect myself more, I find it easier to like others more. I give more freely of myself. I'm less defensive and guarded, more open and respectful of the feelings of others. If you've ever been served poorly in a store, you can probably bet that the server has a few inner conflicts to work out.

Understanding requires openness and empathy, but these efforts carry a risk insecure people can barely afford—the risk of changing opinions, of modifying judgments. Force, coercion, and compulsion will never establish an ideal working and living environment. This comes only through transformation of the inner person, through a life brought into harmony with timeless principles. By sticking to key principles and by consecrating ourselves to noble purposes, we gradually develop a deep internal unity and integrity. Harmony and security replace estrangement and insecurity. Our security comes from within, not from without, not from what others think of us or our social station or material possessions.

The test of the quality of any relationship is found in the little things of every day, the little courtesies, acts of kindness, the give-and-take in little moments. We show our true character in the small things, when we are not on guard. In the seemingly insignificant matters and the simplest habits, we often see egotism come to the surface.

Many human-relations formulas are sunshine philosophies, which sound simple and work when environmental conditions are free of storms. However, unless they work on the roots of character, they only tranquilize and anesthetize. Relationships will buckle when the storms move in. People may then lose their tempers, condemn, criticize, take out hostilities on others, withdraw in indifference, or even turn on themselves.

We all need love, understanding, and acceptance, but fearing we may not receive such warmth, we learn to play roles and defend ourselves against being hurt, to guard our communication, to stand behind facades, to elevate ourselves artificially above others by judging and labeling them. Because of this behavior pattern, we do not receive the love we need, even though others may try to give it to us.

Our role in relationships is to be a light, not a judge. We hear a great deal as to how to overcome insecurity and inferiority and how to acquire confidence and inner peace. However, few advice givers work on the roots of the human character and the laws and plan of life. Self-alienation is the root cause of relationship breakdowns.

Our cultural models may teach us to exploit and manipulate relationships, to defend our pride, to hurt before being hurt, to suspect and doubt, to pretend and take shortcuts, to take a lot and give little, to gratify our appetites and selfish desires and interests, even at the expense of others, if necessary. But as we rise above the negative cultural norms and follow higher moral laws, we increasingly free ourselves from this cultural conditioning.

CREATE INTIMACY. The key to creating this bonding between parents and children, between customers and suppliers, is a win-win mindset. When you create that bonding, the customer comes to say, "You may know our needs better than we do. We only know what our current needs and wants are. We are blinded, in a sense, by our own forest. You have a larger view of the forest. We will let you deal with our real needs and our anticipated needs, but we will also tell you things you don't know about us, then things you don't know about yourself."

As dialogue develops, more insight comes into the relationship. It is hard once you have bonded with a person or company to just ask, "What's in it for me?" The more you bond, the more you care. You go the second mile for each other. People who are closely bonded in a reciprocal relationship can't be selfish. Bonding and selfishness are mutually exclusive concepts.

SHARE KNOWLEDGE AND INFORMATION. Be willing to share information and share problems and challenges with each other and try to understand each other and look for ways to help each other. Engage in dialogue: "I can see you are struggling with getting the cost down in this area. Here's what we have learned . . ."

"We are also having difficulty with this. What have you learned?" It's mostly through human communication and seeking to understand each other that the relationship is nurtured.

I asked a group of CEOs, "How many of you are doing 360-degree performance feedback or assessment?" Most of them were, which was very unusual. They were outstanding leaders. For most of them, there is no disconnect between shareholder relations and stock value, between employee relations and bottom-line returns. They're all integrated together. They know it's an ecosystem. Today's world is making supplier-customer interdependency all the more apparent.

INCLUDE ALL STAKEHOLDER RELATIONSHIPS. If you focus only on one stakeholder to the exclusion of others, you may move away from total stakeholder satisfaction to total customer satisfaction at the expense of employees. Effective managers wouldn't think of taking advantage of their employees because they are their suppliers. All of us are suppliers and customers. I'm a supplier to my customers, and I'm a customer to my suppliers. I meet your needs as you meet my needs. In the final analysis, business is all about relationships. Sure, there's a technical side to business, but I think it is better to deal with the needs of people—all stakeholders. There are no small people. I sometimes encounter a company that has tremendous relationships with customers, but then they treat suppliers terribly. They compartmentalize things. They kill the goose that lays the golden egg by polluting the environment, penalizing the next generation, or ignoring the needs of the society around them.

CARE ABOUT THOSE ON THE FRONT LINES. The frontline service providers, those who tend to be abused and used and unappreciated by management, are the keys to success in any service organization. So, what do you do to cultivate that relationship so that they provide exceptional service? The same principle of reciprocity applies. You realize that person is in the middle, in the crossfire, between the demands of the customers and the operational policies of management. They are really in no-man's-land, and they need to be understood and appreciated. I've seen flight attendants on airplanes, for example, shed tears and share sad stories in the back of the plane after they are treated poorly, then grow calloused by the sheer numbers of people they are processing.

General Colin Powell once described a particular general's leadership style: "He was a tough overseer. The job got done, but by coercion, not motivation. Staff conferences turned into harangues. Inspections became inquisitions. The endless negative pressure exhausted the unit commanders and staff." In sharp contrast, the leadership style of General Bernard Loeffke, a colleague and mentor of Colin Powell, created a great *esprit de corps* that invigorated the troops. In Vietnam, Loeffke rewarded the top performers in his unit by allowing one man each night to sleep in his tent as he took his place on the front lines. Who would not fight for such a leader?

CHOOSE MERCY OVER "MEASURE FOR MEASURE." In his plays *Measure for Measure* and *The Merchant of Venice*, Shakespeare explores the moral dilemmas of exacting "a pound of flesh" and of taking a measure for measure. Near the end of *Merchant*, the fair Portia poetically expresses the virtue of mercy: "The quality of mercy is not strained; it droppeth as the gentle rain from heaven upon the place beneath. It is twice blest; it blesseth him that gives and him that takes: 'Tis mightiest in the mightiest; it becomes the throned monarch better than his crown: His scepter shows the force of temporal power, the attribute to awe and majesty, wherein doth sit the dread and fear of kings; but mercy is above this sceptered sway; it is enthroned in the hearts of kings, it is an attribute to God himself, and earthly power doth then show likest God's when mercy seasons justice. . . . In the course of justice, none of us should see salvation: we do pray for mercy; and that same prayer doth teach us all to render the deeds of mercy."

Recognize that others need love and understanding and mercy just as you do. These simple principles, consistently applied, ensure the kind of bonding that leads to primary greatness.

Customers to the Rescue

In some cases in which there is a reciprocal relationship, customers have rallied to support, even save, a company in need.

Many years ago, Pan American World Airways began to flounder in the marketplace. I knew of several lifelong customers who felt deep loyalty to Pan Am and wanted to help the company in financial trouble. Some tried to help, while others merely took advantage of last-minute measures and offers to fly at deep discounts. Company leaders never really organized and rallied customer support, perhaps underestimating the value of the equity built up over the years in the Emotional Bank Accounts of people over countless flights.

Occasionally, we see business leaders in trouble become very open and honest with their stakeholders in the hope that they will jump in to save them. Sadly, when their companies recover, these leaders often forget the people and the principles that saved them.

We see the same thing in politics when elected officials first dip in the polls, then receive some saving grace from voters who give them a second chance, only to return to their old ways.

Reciprocal relationships provide a healthy return on investment. Sacrifice pays. You always reap as you sow in the long run. It's a universal law. Sacrifice so affects the hearts of other people that it will usually come back to you tenfold. Again, there are only two relationships in business: customer and supplier. All of us play both roles all the time on both an internal and external basis. The very essence of business is relationships. If those are firmly based on principles, they produce their own fruit. Charity never fails.

The law of reciprocity is just as constant as the law of gravity. You can't violate a moral principle or a natural law without suffering the consequence. We all have the balance of our daily operations paid over to us at the end of every minute of our lives.

You may cheat your customers, your children, or your constituents for a while, but nature is never deceived. She credits and debits according to merit. The law of reciprocity is just as constant as the law of gravity. You can't violate a principle or a natural law without suffering the consequences. We all have the balance of our daily operations paid over to us at the end of every minute of our lives.

Application & Suggestions

> Write your answers: Our ability to get along well with others flows naturally from how well we get along with ourselves. "When I like and respect myself more, I find it easier to like others more. I give more freely of myself. I'm less defensive and guarded, more open and respectful of the feelings of others." How do you get along with yourself? Where do you have trouble? What steps could you take to improve your feelings about yourself?

> "The test of the quality of any relationship is found in the little things of every day, the little courtesies, acts of kindness, the give-and-take in little moments." Write in your journal: What *small* steps can you take today to improve a key relationship at work and at home? Take those steps and record the results.

CHAPTER 14

THE LEVER OF DIVERSITY

It is time for parents to teach young people early on that
in diversity there is beauty and there is strength.

—MAYA ANGELOU

People of secondary greatness tend to clone themselves; they surround themselves with people like them, they listen only to opinions that agree with their own, and they have trouble tolerating differences of opinion, background, education, experience, and so on. Sameness holds you down and drains your energy. Primary greatness seeks out diversity. Nothing kills success faster than being incapaci-

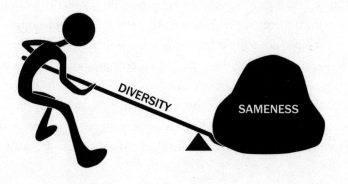

tated by limited data and narrow thinking. Without diversity, there is no synergy and, without synergy, nothing new happens.

I see a negative synergy in many organizations today, as people struggle in teams to deal with differences and maintain positive, productive relationships. Often the negative dynamics in their relationships kill creative potential. They wonder how to turn those relationships around to get more creative, innovative thinking and positive results. The key is to stop cloning yourself and to start valuing diversity.

The natural tendency is to surround ourselves with people like us instead of creating a complementary team. Cloning yourself produces negative energy, because it inhibits other people's talents and gifts. On the other hand, building a complementary team—which has one goal but many different roles, perceptions, methods, and approaches—enables the full expression of talents, and releases positive energy.

Why is the tendency to clone so prevalent and so strong? It is because cloning gives leaders a false sense of security. When you have people thinking like you, doing like you, speaking like you, referring to you, quoting you, dressing like you, and grooming like you, then you feel that you're being validated as a leader. You feel that you have value because other people value being like you. However, they're telling you what you want to hear, not what you need to know. So you may get some artificial harmony, conformity, or uniformity, but you won't have much creativity, synergy, unity, or security. Cloning comes from insecurity and from being centered on public opinion.

Economic necessity teaches that same principle to many companies. In fact, I see that diversity and synergy are being championed by most major organizations today. When I read their reports or listen to their leaders, I hear them all talking about teams, diversity, synergy, and innovation. These principles are vital to bottom-line performance in the global marketplace. More leaders are realizing that nothing kills success more than being incapacitated by limited data and narrow thinking.

They see that sameness is not oneness, uniformity is not unity. The new ideal is the complementary team where unity is achieved by those who have different talents—who have one vision and purpose but many roles, perceptions, capacities, and duties. My experience suggests that unless you have a transcendent purpose and a shared value system, differences become negative and counterproductive—not positive and synergistic—simply because there isn't unity on the fundamentals. If there's unity on the fundamentals, you can tolerate differences in other areas and still have positive synergy.

In his classic book *A Guide for the Perplexed*, Eric Schumacher talks about convergent and divergent problems. A convergent problem is like a problem in a car. If you have a mechanical problem, it's just a matter of checking this and that until your diagnostic process converges on the problem. With a divergent problem, however, the more you study it, the farther apart the views get, the greater the differences of opinion become, and the higher the likelihood for failure, unless there is a transcendent purpose.

> *Cloning gives leaders a false sense of security. When you have people thinking like you, doing like you, speaking like you, referring to you, quoting you, dressing like you, and grooming like you, then you feel that you're being validated as a leader. You feel that you have value because other people value being like you. But they're telling you what you want to hear, not what you need to know.*

He illustrates this principle with the French motto: "Liberty, Equality, Fraternity." If you push the concepts of equality and liberty far enough, you'll find that they are divergent values—they go in opposite directions. Equality means everyone is treated as if they are the same, while liberty means everyone has the right to be different. The higher value is fraternity. So if love or fraternity is your transcendent value, there is no conflict between liberty and equality.

Schumacher says that when you encounter a divergent problem, you need to find some higher purpose to which you can attach to the problem. You can then get back to positive synergy.

For example, my wife and I met with a builder and an architect some time ago to discuss a matter. I asked the builder, "What do you think about the architect's idea for the project?" And he said, "I think it's fine." I said, "How do you feel about it?" He said, "Well, if he feels that's okay, I feel fine about it." I said, "Now, how do you really feel about it?" And he said, "Well, I feel pretty good, I guess." I said, "Well, then we don't need you anymore." He said, "What do you mean?" I said, "When two agree, one's unnecessary. There's no synergy. Until you honestly express your ideas, we won't get your best thinking or achieve team synergy."

After that, the positive energy in our meetings increased dramatically, because we fully expressed ourselves. Different opinions were viewed positively. We all had the same purpose; although we saw things differently, we each brought something unique to the project. Those unique differences become a strength, enabling synergistic alternatives that are better than our original ideas.

Security Breeds Synergy

Whether you're building a house, designing a product, providing a service, or improving a marriage, the principle of valuing differences to achieve synergy applies.

If we buy in to this principle, why don't we practice it more often? The primary reason we often fail to achieve synergy in our projects and relationships is because our personal security is threatened by differences. Our security is fragile if it is based on the need to be right.

At the root of the ability to fully value and celebrate difference in others is having your own personal security tied to a shared vision, common purpose, and integrity based on principles. If your security lies there, you can improvise, adapt, flow, change, and easily admit, "I was wrong," because you're not taking the whole thing personally. You can then be very positive and supportive.

My son Joshua once tried out for the quarterback position on the freshman football team at his high school. He talked to me one day about how his confidence was a product of his performance. I told him, "Your performance will be a product of your confidence if your confidence does not come from football but from living correct principles—being very caring about your team members, working as a team, improving daily, being very honest with the coaches, and learning to value differences to achieve positive energy and synergy on the team."

I wasn't sure if he was even listening, but in a game a week later, another boy who was trying out for starting quarterback was being criticized by the coaches for his performance in the first half. In the locker room at halftime, the boy broke down. He didn't even want to play the second half.

My son later told me: "I didn't really want to come into the game. He's my close friend, and I cared about him. But then, I also cared about the team and doing the best I could do."

He talked with his friend and coaches about creating a situation where his friend's strengths—speed, power, and size—could be complemented by his own strengths—agility and passing ability. He did this because he cared so much about his friend as a person and wanted to build him up.

We all need to base our identity, security, and confidence on something other than our performance, position, or public opinion. If we share a common vision and mission, we can build our identity on the transcendent purpose that unites us, as well as on correct principles. We need both purpose and principles, vision and values. If our mission statement is only about principles, we may be good, but good for what? And if we have vision without principles or values, we may rise to the top, but we will take many people down with us when the inevitable crash comes.

Albert E. Gray, a legendary insurance executive, spent his life trying to find what he called the "common denominator of success." Finally, he came to this: "The secret of success of every man who has ever been successful lies in the fact that he formed the habit of doing things that failures don't like to do."[11] Successful people don't like doing them either, necessarily. But their dislike is subordinated to the strength of their purpose.

> *We all need to base our identity, security, and confidence on something other than our performance, position, or public opinion. If we share a common vision and mission, we can build our identity on the transcendent purpose that unites us, as well as on correct principles.*

Everyone who seeks primary greatness needs to have an inspiring vision and a transcendent purpose. They must avoid getting hung up on their perceptions or their methods, but to value differences as people meet together to come up with a way of doing things.

One day, when I left a board meeting of my company, I realized the thing that united us was a common purpose. All members expressed their opinions, and there was strong disagreement on methods proposed to accomplish the aims. But I detected no negative energy in that meeting.

If we share a transcending purpose, common vision, and shared mission in our relationships, we can afford to have many differences, and they'll become strengths. We actually want them, because if we don't have them, then we'll always be limited by incomplete data and a partial perspective. You'll only have your view, your history, your value system, and this will be the lens through which you see everything in your corporation or marriage.

Twenty-first century business demands that we get involvement, listen to our people, listen to our customers, and set up partnerships. All those processes essentially involve diversity, appreciating differences.

Fruits of Positive Synergy

The wonderful fruits of synergy include improved products, services, and relationships. You see that the whole is greater than the sum of the parts. You have true creative cooperation that produces things no one could ever have achieved alone. You give a small group a heroic goal that looks totally impossible from every point of view, have them go to work on it, and they'll come up with new ways of thinking about it.

Another benefit of synergy is that it bonds people. Anytime you and I have a creative experience, where we produce something together that was not there before, that memory is bonding.

Have you ever had a creative experience with your kids? What impact did that have on your relationship? When I have my one-on-one dates with my kids, I have an open agenda. They write the agenda, and we do something that is unique and fun; in fact, my daughter Colleen has several journals full of her daddy-daughter experiences.

Another great benefit of synergy is that it builds a cultural immune system. We become immune to problems or differences because the culture already has its own T cells and white cells. It knows it can fight divisiveness because it's fought it and won before.

A Final Caution

A wise father once counseled his son about seeking a marriage partner: "You want as many similarities as you can find, because there will be enough differences anyway." There is some truth to that. I see companies going out of their way to seek differences, to champion the diversity cause, but then have a real problem with divisiveness because they don't have basic commonalities.

The most important commonalities deal with your philosophy, your purpose, your value system, and your perception—not with race, religion, gender, or nationality. For instance, if you and your spouse didn't have the same basic purpose with your kids, the different ways you approach child-rearing issues could tear your marriage apart. Even with a common vision and mission, you'll still have your struggles communicating on those issues; but eventually, if you're both focused on the higher value, you'll come up with a 3rd Alternative, or else one will say, "Well, it's not that important to me; let's do it your way."

> *The secret of success of every man who has ever been successful lies in the fact that he formed the habit of doings things that failures don't like to do.*
>
> *—Albert E. Gray*

Many companies struggle as they adopt diversity programs because the leaders, while self-aware enough to know they need to be more diverse, make careless hiring and promotion decisions. If you go for diversity for the sake of diversity, you may get tokenism, or worse, a total bombshell where people aren't prepared for key assignments. That which we desire most earnestly, we believe most easily. And if we desire diversity so earnestly that we grab it whenever and wherever we find it, we'll have more divisiveness than synergy.

My point here is that there are elastic limits to diversity. There needs to be real commonality on core issues, not just difference for difference's sake. There must be commonality on purpose and values and, hopefully, those values are based on principles. The ultimate source of security comes from integrity toward these higher purposes and principles.

Application & Suggestions

> Write in your journal: What are the dangers of having a team of clones who think, act, and look alike? What examples of these dangers have you personally seen?
> In a complementary team, unity is achieved by people who have different talents—who have one vision and purpose, but many roles, perceptions, capacities, and duties. What can you do to make your own work team more complementary? Whose talents are being neglected? What kind of groupthink is holding you back? Where do you have talent gaps in your team?
> Write your answers: Describe an unusually creative or synergistic experience you have had. What role did others play in that experience? How can you re-create the conditions that led to that kind of synergy?

CHAPTER 15

THE LEVER OF LEARNING

Anyone who stops learning is old, whether at twenty or
eighty. Anyone who keeps learning stays young.

—HENRY FORD

Secondary greatness isn't very interested in learning, but primary
greatness demands it. In business, a person who isn't constantly up-
grading his or her skills and knowledge becomes untrustworthy in
time. Beyond this, learning is what we call a *primary good*, valuable
for its own sake. The love of learning and the search for wisdom help
make life worthwhile. We all have a moral obligation to the people

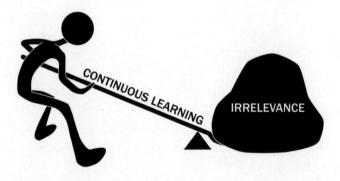

who are important in our lives, as well as to ourselves, to learn and progress without ceasing.

We often talk of the need for continuing education in the context of work, but we rarely speak of it as a governing principle of life. In fact, continuous learning will save your life because, without it, you slip quickly into irrelevance.

I would argue that separate and apart from our jobs, we all have an obligation to learn and progress. And lifelong learning is not so much about big campaigns, programs, academic degrees, and credentials, as it is about short daily study sessions and small doses of appropriate on-the-job training. Pushing the learning lever a little bit each day keeps you sharp and relevant.

The principle of balance is key to continuous learning. I recommend a balance between personal and organizational development; between current job-related needs and future requirements; between industry-related learning and general education. Make sure your approach is systematic and based on feedback to you—personally and professionally. Your learning should balance theory with practice; arts with the sciences.

> *We all have a moral obligation to learn and progress. And lifelong learning is not so much about big campaigns, programs, academic degrees, and credentials, as it is about short daily study sessions and small doses of relevant on-the-job training.*

In addition, make sure your learning and development are motivated by a desire to be of greater service. Such virtuous intent, as philosopher Adam Smith observed in his book *The Theory of Moral Sentiments,* is central to primary greatness. Far too many organizations exploit a person's knowledge and training without investing in that knowledge and training; likewise, many individuals exploit the training and education opportunities offered by their organizations.

Such hit-and-run activity is expensive for both parties. Thus, there is a mutual responsibility. Organizations make a tremendous investment in the learning and development of human resources. I believe that individuals who take advantage of corporate training programs ought to supply returns on the investment. Adam Smith talks about the virtuous energies that must be exercised by individuals and organizations. Both must feel a mutual responsibility for each other. If the free-enterprise system is to function properly, Smith observed, all economic relations must be based on virtue and caring one for another.

Corporate Responsibility

As I assess the needs of corporations, I clearly see that we simply can't compete without creating a culture of continuous learning, with knowledge workers who are continually enhancing skills and updating technology.

My guess is that about 20 percent of the present work force is obsolete. And in another ten years, another 20 percent could be obsolete if we don't overcome the cultural norm that education ends when our schooling ends. We need a deep commitment to both personal and professional development on a continuous basis.

Horst Schulze, cofounder of The Ritz-Carlton Hotel Company, advocates daily training. He believes that people need to learn something new every day. At their properties, they have short on-the-job training sessions daily, and most of those sessions are interactive dialogue involving the entire workforce. Every day, hotel managers adapt the messages they receive from the corporate office to the needs of their people. Such systematic training of the whole workforce should be highly commended. Yet, I imagine Horst Schulze often hears the argument that such training is too costly. However, given the white-water world in which we live, the far greater cost, without question, is *not* to do it. I think that any cost-benefit analysis would come down on the side of continuous training and education.

Still, many of us simply don't see the value of continuous learning. Most executives are not invested in systematic training and development. And because they're not invested, their people, their products, and their organizations are in danger of becoming obsolete; they also become insecure as the competitive environment makes their organization obsolete.

Security today no longer lies in the old psychological contract of lifetime employment. Security lies in the ability to continue to produce what the marketplace wants, and those wants are constantly changing. Unless people learn, change, grow, and progress to accommodate the market, there can be no security. Security lies in the power to continually learn.

Personal Responsibility

The individual must take personal responsibility for professional development, not leaving it to the organization. The proactive person will see the organization as a resource and fount of information about what would be most relevant to learn. But the individual must make it happen.

As proactive individuals take more responsibility for their own learning and professional development, they begin to see the organization as a supplementary resource. They do not transfer primary responsibility to the organization. They do not expect their organizations to freely provide all the learning and training needed for them to excel in their jobs; however, they take full advantage of relevant training when it is offered, and they pay back their organizations by making significant contributions.

A business can only do so much; the rest is up to the individual. As individuals, we ought to take into account the needs of the organization in our personal- and professional-development programs; otherwise, we may be developing for the wrong reason or at the wrong time. Our personal development should be relevant to the economy, to the industry, to the company, and to our current assignment.

However, we also need to develop in a general sense to avoid becoming obsolete if our company or function becomes obsolete. If our development is too job-related, we are more vulnerable to market forces. While we need to be competent specialists in our current jobs, we also need to start and maintain a personal general-education program.

I believe that is best done in one- to two-hour sessions every day of our working life. We also need approximately one day a month in training that is systematic and conceptually aligned not only with our present job, but also with our future contributions. I schedule myself for training about one day a month, and I also set aside one to two hours every day for general education.

Development Options

Among the many job-related learning options available to most people are the following.

> **RESEARCH SKILLS OF ANALYSIS AND SYNTHESIS.** Knowledge workers, even on the factory floor, need to hone their thinking skills, especially in the areas of gathering, analyzing, and synthesizing data. Data analytics is one of the top necessary skills of this century. For instance, on one particular project in our company, some superficial analysis was done that suggested a huge market for a new product. However, one person who was well trained in analytics reached

a different conclusion in a matter of hours. It soon became evident that there was not a big market for that particular product at all.

› **PERSONAL READING PROGRAM.** The education and training you received in the distant past doesn't suffice. Keep current in business by reading *Harvard Business Review, Fortune,* and other publications that provide in-depth analysis. I also recommend reading some weekly business magazines and newspapers like *Businessweek* and *The Wall Street Journal;* also, make sure you skim the most respected periodicals in science, economics, politics, and the arts. Key social-media sites provide fast and thought-provoking analysis of the business world. Reviewing the best new business and leadership books is also vital.

› **REVIEW OF CLASSIC LITERATURE.** Another part of your personal learning program should be exposure to great literature. I feel that I cheated myself in my undergraduate studies, and I have tried to compensate over the years. Two of my children majored in English and studied great classic literature. I can see how it has given them perspective and wisdom.

› **PERSONAL UNIVERSITIES.** Create your own personal university. Go to the Internet and find TED talks and MOOCs (massive open online courses) that can enrich your learning and provide you with important insights. Join book clubs online or in person. In today's world, every proactive person can take personal responsibility for learning and professional development, and set up their own private university by becoming their own curriculum designer.

Application & Suggestions

> Are you committed to both personal and professional development on a continuous basis? Write your answers: Where do you need to improve your knowledge or skills? What are the barriers to this effort? How can you take down those barriers? What opportunities could you take advantage of to increase your learning? Set a learning goal or milestone: "By this date, I will be certified in _____," or "By that date, I will complete an online course in _____."

> Create your own personal university with the rich resources available to you online. Set a process goal for making your learning continuous. Which sites, periodicals, podcasts, or conferences do you need to keep up with at all times? Set up bookmarks for sites you should track, and plan time each week to check in with those sources.

CHAPTER 16

THE LEVER OF RENEWAL

Words are like eggs dropped from great heights. You could no more call them back than ignore the mess they left when they fell.

—STEPHEN R. COVEY

You can't achieve primary greatness by neglecting yourself—your health, your mind, your emotional and spiritual life. Each of these vital areas of your life needs constant, even daily, renewal. Pushing the lever a little bit every day can offset a slow or even catastrophic downward decline in your personal energy and even save your life.

Many years ago, I began teaching the principle of daily and

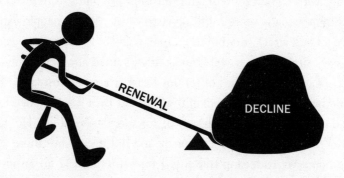

weekly renewal to students and business managers. That principle became codified in my book *The 7 Habits of Highly Effective People* as Habit 7: Sharpen the Saw. Abraham Lincoln said, "If I only had two hours to chop down a tree, I would spend the first hour sharpening my ax." There are many versions of this quotation, but the principle holds true. Such wisdom may be axiomatic, and yet we see many people who are so busy sawing (working, producing, performing, doing) that they never (or very seldom) stop to sharpen the saw (rest, recreate, study, prepare, reflect, rethink, retool, revitalize); nor do they invest in a new, high-technology power saw. Instead, they work with ineffective tools: poor social skills and a dull mind, dissipated body, and weakened spirit.

Four Assumptions

I encourage people to act on four assumptions dealing with the four parts of human nature: physical, mental, social, and spiritual. The ultimate personal synergy comes when we renew ourselves in all four dimensions regularly, on both personal and professional levels.

PHYSICAL ASSUMPTION: IMAGINE YOU HAVE ALREADY HAD ONE HEART ATTACK (PERSONAL) OR ONE BUSINESS FAILURE (PROFESSIONAL). Work on the assumption that you should live carefully, wisely, with a good exercise and nutrition program, so that you can have many, many more fulfilling years of life. When people experience a heart attack, most of them make radical lifestyle changes.

For example, my friend Gene Dalton gained another twenty-five years of life after a series of serious heart attacks almost killed him while he studied and taught at the Harvard Business School. He altered his lifestyle completely, opting for a less stressful job. He transferred to Brigham Young University and did twenty-five more years of productive leadership training. I once met him at an airport in

Atlanta, where he was walking up and down the concourse between flights. Daily exercise made a big difference in his life; he also ate carefully. It took a lot of discipline, but he was highly motivated, because the alternative was worse.

MENTAL ASSUMPTION: IMAGINE THAT YOUR KNOWLEDGE (PERSONAL) AND SKILLS (PROFESSIONAL) WILL BE OBSOLETE WITHIN THREE YEARS. If you make this assumption—and it is accurate, by the way—you will get into serious systematic study and reading; you won't just stay within your own narrow interests, specialty, or comfort zone. You will leave your comfort zone and read and think broadly and widely and deeply about your field, and also about the disruptive forces that are changing the world right under your feet. You have to learn to think strategically so you can examine the assumptions and paradigms underlying your field, because these could be made obsolete by some new paradigm, process, or product. Hit-and-miss learning and extrinsic motivation that comes from listening to a few podcasts or audiobooks may be useful but insufficient. I recommend that you read several periodicals outside your own field—publications that challenge your thinking; perhaps four a month. Keep expanding your scope and horizon. Read substantive articles from the most respected online sources, periodicals, and books.

As you look at your own career, note that there are real hazards down the road, and that fatal career accidents can and do happen. Take preventive measures now. Prepare well for the future you want.

SOCIAL ASSUMPTION: IMAGINE THAT EVERYTHING YOU SAY ABOUT OTHER PEOPLE WILL BE HEARD BY THEM, BOTH AT HOME (PERSONAL) AND AT WORK (PROFESSIONAL). You might still be critical, but your criticism will be far more responsible and constructive when you feel as if they are listening to what you say. Why not operate all the time on this assumption? If you want to retain the trust of those who are present and be loyal to those who are absent, remember this: He who lives by the sword of criticism dies by the sword of criticism. Irresponsible criticism and backbiting weakens character in the person and in the culture.

I once read in *Scientific American* that scientists are developing the technology to recover sound. That gives new meaning to the old proverb about idle words: Every idle word you speak shall be shouted upon the housetops. The moment that you start applying this principle, it causes you to become more responsible in all of your relationships, and that will have a salutary effect on everything and everyone with whom you interact.

SPIRITUAL ASSUMPTION: IMAGINE THAT YOU WILL SOON HAVE A ONE-ON-ONE ACCOUNTING WITH THE PEOPLE YOU LOVE AND WHO LOVE YOU (PERSONAL) AND WITH YOUR BOSS AND TEAM MEMBERS (PROFESSIONAL). In this personal interview, you will give an accounting of your stewardship: how well you are maintaining your physical health and fitness; what you have learned and how well you have employed knowledge and skills; how true and loyal you are to other people, especially behind their backs; and how well you are developing the spiritual side of your nature. Assume also that you have a similar stewardship interview scheduled soon with your boss and those with whom you work. Of course, you probably already have something like an annual performance appraisal now, but this 360-degree evaluation would also take into account your own feelings about your job performance, the key question being, "What have you done with what you had to work with?"

> *He who lives by the sword of criticism dies by the sword of criticism. Irresponsible criticism and backbiting weakens character in the person and in the culture.*

Powerful Advantages

Why are these four assumptions so powerful? If you behave accordingly, you will start putting first things first. Why? You will experience a massive Paradigm Shift, and you will see the whole situation differently. Changing your paradigm is more powerful than trying to change your behavior or your attitude. If you operate on all four assumptions, you will find that they are closely interrelated. As you take care of the physical side, you improve the climate for innovative thinking. And as you behave as if everything you say will be heard by others, you improve not only your relationships but also spiritual health. Each assumption also brings its own reward.

PHYSICAL. Your preventive health measures will not only extend your life but improve the quality of your life. You will feel better longer and extend your prime time for performance. Many healthy seniors do their best work and leave a lasting legacy during the final years of their lives.

MENTAL. Your ongoing study and learning will prepare you for future opportunities. Continuous learning will keep you in control, even with all the changes in the economy. However, if you stop learning, especially in areas vital to your career path, you will soon be obsolete. You will likely adopt a victim mindset and start blaming your organization. However, the reality is that you can't add value because your skillset has become obsolete.

SOCIAL. You will gain more empathy and achieve more synergy in your social and professional relationships. Your concern for the name and reputation of other people will enable you to see things from their point of view, and to seek first to understand. You will also gain the courage and conviction necessary to express how you see things and seek to be understood by others so that, together, you can accomplish worthwhile purposes and projects.

SPIRITUAL. You will experience inner peace and new confidence in your capabilities. Acting as though your life could end at any moment will encourage you to do the right thing in the moment of choice. When you make the conscious choice to do the right thing, you gain inner peace. And as an added benefit, you will gain new confidence in your capabilities. Constant renewal will keep you competent to serve at the highest level of your personal and professional pursuits.

Application & Suggestions

> Write in your journal your response to each of these scenarios:
>> Imagine you have already had one serious heart attack. What would you change?
>> What would you do if you knew your knowledge would be obsolete in three years?
>> How would your conversation change if you knew everything you said about other people could be heard by them?
>> Assume you will soon have a one-on-one accounting with your boss and team members. How would you answer the question "What have you done with what you had to work with?"
> Consider the best ways to Sharpen the Saw: rest, recreate, study, prepare, reflect, rethink, retool, revitalize. How can you make these into daily and weekly priorities? Set aside time in your weekly plan to Sharpen the Saw in these four need areas: physical, social-emotional, mental, and spiritual.

CHAPTER 17

THE LEVER OF TEACHING

If you want to build a ship, don't drum up people together to collect wood and don't assign them tasks and work, but rather teach them to long for the endless immensity of the sea.

—ANTOINE DE SAINT-EXUPÉRY

What's the best way to internalize the levers of primary greatness you've just learned about? It's simple: Teach them to others. As you do, your understanding of the levers will deepen. Others will look to you to exemplify those principles. You'll become an authority on primary greatness.

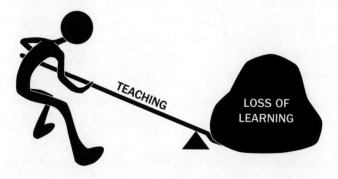

This story starts in 1975, when I took a course from Dr. Walter A. Gong, a visiting professor from San Jose State University, on how to improve teaching. His basic lesson was simply this: The best way to learn something is to teach it. I was impressed that Dr. Gong practiced this principle daily with his family. Each night at dinner, Dr. Gong asked his sons, Gerrit and Brian, and daughter Marguerite to teach the essence of what they had learned that day in school. And the result? All three children became Rhodes Scholars who received their Ph.D.s from Oxford, Stanford, and the Fletcher School of Law and Diplomacy.

Now, most people already know the truth of this principle. It is self-evident. Still, it is not used much in business, or even in education. And yet, the single most important thing I have learned in the field of training and development is to teach what you learn to others.

> *Everyone has to be upgraded in knowledge and skills. We all have to go back to school. The new emphasis on training and education, on upgrading the mindset and skillset of everyone, comes in response to the demands of the global economy.*

Dr. Gong's learning process involved three roles for every learner: (1) capturing or understanding essential information, (2) expanding or applying this knowledge into his own life for his own purposes and values, and (3) teaching others for their benefit and growth. Since growth increases dramatically when people teach what they learn to others, each person must see himself or herself as both learner and teacher in all areas of responsibility and accountability.

When I started pushing on this simple lever in the mid-1970s, my own learning accelerated dramatically and my teaching improved. I found ways not only to teach more students, but also to reach a much wider audience with greater impact.

At the university, I started teaching small classes of twenty to twenty-five students, but ended up teaching from five hundred to one thousand students per semester. My teacher-student ratio went from one to one thousand. Then teaching to learn enabled me to reduce that ratio to one-to-one. In most cases, student scores rose higher than ever. Most of my students actually learned more in a class of one thousand than in a group of twenty, because they were teaching each other one-on-one.

My colleagues and I have also applied this practice in our workshops, asking people to teach each other what they have learned. This short exercise gives participants a sense of the accelerated learning that is possible, and it makes a big difference in what they learn and apply. Again, you simply learn more when you know you have to teach others.

How to Capture Learning

Most people have not cultivated the ability to capture and express the essence of what they learn. Dr. Gong taught how to capture by taking notes under five headings.

PURPOSE: Try to discern the significant purpose of the teacher or presenter. Even if he or she is not well organized or skilled, you can organize your mind and notes in this way by asking, "What is the presenter's purpose?"

MAIN POINTS: What are the main points or central messages?

VALIDATION: What evidence or examples were presented? How did the person validate his or her points?

APPLICATION: How can these points be applied to life?

VALUE: How much value did the teacher put on this learning?

Four Advantages of Teaching to Learn

I see four big advantages in applying this principle.

YOU SIMPLY LEARN BETTER WHEN YOU TEACH. The main reason you learn better when you teach is because your paradigm has shifted. When you see yourself as a teacher, you take a far more responsible attitude toward learning. You are far more motivated to learn something when you know you are responsible to teach it. You see yourself not only as a listener and learner, but also as a teacher and mentor. So you become a much better learner.

WHEN YOU TEACH SOMETHING YOU FEEL GOOD ABOUT, YOU INCREASE THE LIKELIHOOD OF LIVING BY IT. By teaching something, you make a social statement. It makes you accountable along with the people you teach. They now expect you to live by it. Teaching creates a kind of social support system, a social expectation, or an implied social contract. If you live what you teach, you are much more credible—and your teaching becomes much more inspiring and motivating.

WHEN YOU TEACH WHAT YOU LEARN, YOU PROMOTE BONDING IN THE RELATIONSHIP. People who have been influenced by great teachers tend to feel very close to them. Note how much appreciation and respect they give their teachers. Also, note how the teacher reciprocates when a student really cares about the material. There is a deepened relationship in teaching that bonds people.

WHEN YOU TEACH SOMETHING THAT YOU ARE LEARNING, IT LUBRICATES THE CHANGE AND GROWTH PROCESS FOR YOURSELF. It makes change legitimate as you see yourself (and others see you) in a new light; and when you begin to see yourself in a new light, you experi ence more and faster growth. If you teach me something that you recently learned and experienced, I will be more open to both the message and the messenger. I might also share something relevant with you that I learned. We both change and grow.

Of course, you need to recognize that there's a time to teach and a time not to teach. It's time to teach when (1) people are not threatened—trying to teach when people feel threatened will only increase resentment, so wait for or create a new situation in which the person feels more secure and receptive; (2) you're not angry or frustrated, when you have feelings of affection, respect, and inward security; and (3) when the other person needs help and support. (To rush in with success formulas when someone is emotionally low or fatigued or under a lot of pressure is comparable to trying to teach a drowning man to swim.)

Remember, we are teaching something all the time, because we are constantly radiating who and what we are.

Teaching to Learn Unleashes New Levels of Performance

I have come to believe that this process of teaching and learning unfreezes the old images people have of each other. When those images refreeze, people are able to perform at a new level.

> *Remember, we are teaching something all the time, because we are constantly radiating who and what we are.*

When an ever-increasing number of people start helping each other to fulfill their appointed roles, a positive culture develops. A learning organization is nothing more or less than a group of people who help each other fulfill their respective missions, roles, and goals.

Some people feel that they are exempt from teaching what they learn, either because they are supposed to know it all already or because teaching is a foreign and frightening experience for them.

Some even have a fear of teaching. For example, executives who tend to stay with their developed skillset may see teaching as a new, undeveloped skill and don't want to seem vulnerable.

However, teaching others is one of the best ways to expand your influence with others. Teaching is a proactive behavior. I believe that our basic nature is to act and not be acted upon. Proactive behavior not only enables us to choose our response to circumstances, but it also empowers us to change and even create our circumstances. As we are open to influence from others (teachable), we will have more influence with them (as a teacher). As we involve others (our students or program participants) meaningfully, we will gain more influence with them.

Much of the money spent on training and development is wasted because participants come away with very little take-home value. Most learning evaporates overnight because few learners teach the material to a broader audience. Some people no longer expect that training will increase knowledge and skills, partly because they know they will never be accountable for sharing it.

My promise to you is this: Applying this simple concept of teaching what you learn will pay big dividends.

Application & Suggestions

> › When do you have opportunities to teach at home and at work? Make a plan to teach someone one principle from this book in the next week. Do it. How did it go? How did your own understanding of the principle change?
> › How can you increase your opportunities for teaching to learn? What would be the outcome if you consistently taught these principles to others? How would it affect your own commitment to living by these principles?

CHAPTER 18

A FINAL WORD: GET WISDOM

It is unwise to be too sure of one's own wisdom. It is healthy to be reminded that the strongest might weaken and the wisest might err.

—GANDHI

Today we hear so much about the explosion in information, intelligence, and knowledge, but not much about wisdom. Where the goal of secondary greatness is self-promotion, the goal of primary greatness is wisdom.

We don't always act wisely. As we look around, we see so many people who simply work against their own interests. What causes these distortions in judgment or lapses in wisdom? And how can they be corrected? I here mention six causes and corrections.

The pride of self-referencing. Correction: The humility of submitting to true-north principles.
We know from a study of human history that when people are well-informed and educated (intelligent), they think they are wise, and often they reject the counsels of wiser or more experienced minds. Why? I think it is because they basically turn away from the true-

north consciousness inside them, and that transgression invariably causes imbalance, distortion, confusion, disorientation—and they likely don't even know it until it's too late, particularly if self is the highest reference.

If you always defer to principles rather than your own judgment, that higher standard helps to instill a sense of humility, happiness, teachability, and a willingness to receive objective data from internal and external sources.

One thing I have learned by teaching my 7 Habits over the years is that the acquisition of these habits takes more than a casual reading of the book—it takes consistent effort over a period of a few years before most people reach the point at which the 7 Habits have become second nature to them. Vertigo is a condition of confusion and disorientation, where you lose touch with physical senses. Your basic kinesthetic senses of position, motion, and tension may become confused and disoriented. When you are in this state of vertigo, all the information and data in the world won't be very helpful because you are interpreting it incorrectly. Thus, you tend to become ever more burdened with information overload. I submit that if your orientation is selfish, self-oriented, or self-referenced, you will be in some state of vertigo. You will then slide downward unless you have some solid reference point to pull you back to an objective reality. This is the strength I see in principle-based living.

The folly of relying only on information. Correction: Converting information to wisdom and directed action.
In my lifetime, I have witnessed the well-documented evolution from the Industrial Age to the Information Age. However, I see four parts to the Information Age. The first is raw data or information. Information today costs an astronomically small fraction of what it cost in 1946 when computer technology was introduced. So now, everyone essentially has access to the same huge base of information; information has become a commodity. The second part of the

Information Age is knowledge, where all this information is organized around conceptual schemes and paradigms. The third quarter is systems thinking, whereby bodies of information are organized with a sense of coherence or wholeness. And the fourth quarter is wisdom, as a sense of purpose and principles governs our acquisition of knowledge.

In every organization, wisdom must be manifest in all decisions and actions. This is why, today, people want to work for leaders and companies that have a clear vision and mission, with clear roles and goals, so that their efforts have meaning and direction and value.

The confusion caused by a renaissance of immorality. Correction: The clarity resulting from a renaissance of morality.

As I travel around the world, I can't help but notice an unethical renaissance taking place. This is a time when many people are losing their ethical bearings. They are experiencing the equivalent of ethical vertigo. I've seen examples of both individuals and organizations whereby they think they are heading toward true north while they are actually heading due south.

But I also believe there is an ethical renaissance taking place—a return to principles, as people are asking the deeper questions: *What is my life and work all about? What is really important here? What is my real worth?* As people ask and answer these questions, they often become more rooted and grounded in the natural laws and principles that govern the world.

The discrepancy between the value people place on their performance and the value management places on it. Correction: The objectivity of market value.

The subjective and emotional assessments as to what a person or product is worth often differ from an objective market assessment. I think that one of the toughest issues for managers is when people have a very different perception of their worth and of their contribution to the organization. Since all parties are usually self-justified and often very morally invested in that justification, the best way I see to ultimately resolve this difference is to rely upon the democracy of the marketplace by bringing the marketplace into the world of these individuals. Basically, the manager might say: "Okay, this is what you think you are worth, but this is what the marketplace thinks you are worth." I'm not talking about your financial net worth but about your total contribution. The marketplace refers to all those people with whom you deal professionally. These people constitute your marketplace.

Receiving objective marketplace feedback is a humbling experience for anyone. We experience this constantly. More than 250,000 people have participated in our 7 Habits personal-profile survey, and it's always a humbling experience for them. However, it can also be very affirming because often their self-reported scores are lower than the scores the marketplace gives them. So the assessment reports the good news as well as revealing the blind spots.

The ignorance and apathy that come as a consequence of closed systems. Correction: Make systems as open as possible within the limits of trust.

The cry for more shared information and open systems often leads to an assumption that everybody ought to have access to all data. However, I feel that openness and access are functions of the trust level. The higher the level of trust, the more open you can be. If the trust level is low and you become too open too soon, people might become disoriented. And based on their skewed perspective of your purpose, they might accuse you of wrong motives.

The myopia of using local criteria to assess quality and competitiveness. Correction: Use global competitive criteria.

Business is ultimately pragmatic. You have to meet four pragmatic criteria today to even enter the arena: One is quality; another is low cost, but quality low-cost producers are a dime a dozen. The other two criteria are speed and innovation. Meeting those four criteria requires people to cooperate willingly and creatively with each other to achieve synergy. Of course, cooperation requires the element of trust, which comes from the foundation of trustworthiness.

The path to wisdom is bordered by objective feedback on performance. We rarely find any resistance to the principles of the 7 Habits because they are so self-evident, but the key question is whether these concepts make a substantial impact on the individual and the organization. How do they know they're succeeding? What kind of feedback are they getting?

Find a growth path whereby you build on known strengths and work on known weaknesses. That means you must have a trustworthy feedback process. And don't let it overwhelm you. Once you start progressing along that path, little by little, over time, you will become increasingly aware of your blind spots and increasingly capable of fixing them.

Four Tenets of Wisdom

Here are four basic tenets of wisdom worthy of consideration.

WISDOM IS KNOWING THAT SUSTAINED, POSITIVE CHANGE BEGINS ON THE INSIDE. Transforming a team or family starts at the personal level. Organizational development and change without personal development and change are illusory, even foolish, because the market demands more transparency, more honesty, and more trustworthiness—in short, natural principles of primary greatness.

There must be individual growth, change, and development to make organizational development and change viable. And yet, as I see it, that basic fact is largely ignored. Too many people think of change as coming from the outside. But fundamentally, productive change requires an Inside-Out Approach, not an outside-in approach.

WISDOM REQUIRES BOTH CHARACTER AND COMPETENCE. When we talk about learning and increasing our capacities and competencies, we usually think in terms of technical competence or conceptual competence. We rarely think in terms of social competence or in terms of character. And yet, ultimately, if a person is to bring about meaningful, lasting change or significant improvement, that person will need to cultivate the characteristics of interdependency, empathy, and synergy as well as the qualities of integrity, maturity, and the Abundance Mentality. Why? Because one's character is constantly radiating and communicating. And based on what people read into this largely nonverbal communication, they will either trust or distrust us.

> *Too many people think of change in terms of some outside force acting on internal conditions. But fundamentally, change that results in quality and productivity requires an Inside-Out Approach, not an outside-in approach.*

Our trustworthiness on an individual level and our credibility on an organizational level are directly linked to our character and competence and the degree of wisdom evident in our judgments, decisions, and actions.

Character is composed of *integrity*, the value we place on our promises; *maturity*, the balance between courage and consideration; and *Abundance Mentality*, the idea that there is plenty out there for everybody. These three character traits are as vital in bringing about needed change as are technical, conceptual, and social competence.

Thankfully, we can all improve and progress. The interplay between character and competency can be evolutionary, both in the character and the competency component. So we need not judge and label people, or assume they can't change in these areas. We can develop competence beyond technical and conceptual capability. We can cultivate the ability to think interdependently and systematically about people, processes, technology, and the new rules and realities of the marketplace.

I like what the great author and teacher Marianne Williamson said:

"Our deepest fear is not that we are inadequate. Our deepest fear is that we are powerful beyond measure. It is our light, not our darkness that most frightens us. We ask ourselves, 'Who am I to be brilliant, gorgeous, talented, fabulous?' Actually, who are you not to be? . . . Your playing small does not serve the world. There is nothing enlightened about shrinking so that other people won't feel insecure around you. We are all meant to shine. . . . It's not just in some of us; it's in everyone. And as we let our own light shine, we unconsciously give other people permission to do the same. As we are liberated from our own fear, our presence automatically liberates others." [12]

When you think about it, the fear of comparison keeps our tremendous qualities and potentials locked inside in our nature.

WISDOM IS MANIFEST WHEN CHARACTER AND COMPETENCE OVERLAP. People who are known to be wise have good, solid judgment. Their knowledge is impregnated with principles that do not change. Wisdom or wise judgment—the confluence of character and competence—is a critical component in the quest for quality of life.

Why is this so? There are so many trends and fashions in business thinking. There was Total Quality, then reengineering, then disruptive innovation, and who knows what's next? There is value in all of these trends, but real wisdom is beyond them.

In my mind, what is beyond is simply what is beneath, what is foundational. Purely technical or conceptual solutions to problems may prove necessary but will always be insufficient. What is often lacking is the character side. Without character, you can't have wisdom, in spite of competence. And without wisdom, you simply can't build and maintain an enduring institution, whether it be a marriage, a family, a team, or a company. Now, you may surely build something, but it won't last. About 80 percent of new businesses fail within the first year; only about one in twelve businesses survives a decade.

Increasingly, unconventional wisdom is necessary to deal intelligently with the false dichotomies and true dilemmas of the day. We just can't get by without genuine, character-based and competency-supported wisdom to deal with the vagaries of the marketplace, diverging opinions, tough trade-offs, and tender relationships.

I know of no other time in history when the need for wisdom has been greater than it is today; and this, paradoxically, in the middle of a great Information Age and knowledge explosion. The truth is out: The more technology advances without wisdom, the worse things become. But in wisdom is the greatest leverage of all—a wise person can turn passive knowledge into a great contribution to the world.

WISDOM LIES BEYOND KNOWLEDGE AND INFORMATION. Since we live in an Information Age and knowledge economy where information is becoming more readily available and more of a commodity to be sold at lower and lower costs, the key thing is not only knowledge of your competitors, customers, products, and processes, but also a wisdom that lies beyond knowledge. The great philosopher Alfred North Whitehead said, "In a sense, knowledge shrinks as wisdom grows, for details are swallowed up in principles. The details of knowledge, which are important, will be picked up ad hoc in each avocation of life, but the habit of the active utilization of well-understood principles is the final possession of wisdom."

Ultimately, character growth only comes from bringing our judgment in alignment with correct principles. It is not merely an intellectual endeavor. Primarily, it is an endeavor of orienting the mind, the will, and the soul toward enduring principles. That is what builds integrity.

You might be technically and conceptually competent, so that you understand the big picture and see how all the parts relate to each other, and yet be incapable of working productively with others because you lack certain qualities of character. Only when you have both character and competence, harnessed by wise judgment, will you have the ability to build relationships, to build high-trust cultures, and to build enduring institutions undisturbed by every fickle thing that happens daily in the marketplace.

A Final Word

People ask me why they should care about primary greatness—or about greatness at all. Some feel they already lead a great life and don't see any reason to change it. And I don't dispute that.

But there is something in us that is always calling us to be greater and better than we are. And if we don't listen to that voice, we risk at every moment falling into secondary greatness, where we become limited by the social lens through which we see the world or, even worse, we become fixated on the forces that constrain us and fall victim to an enemy-centered paranoia.

By contrast, the end of a life filled with primary greatness is wisdom—a perspective that embraces principles, continuous growth, and an integrated wholeness. It is a perspective that brings peace to the inner person and prosperity to the world. It is a perspective that brings security because the principles upon which we live our lives are solid, enduring, and will never change.

Application & Suggestions

› If your orientation is selfish, self-oriented, or self-referenced, you will be in some state of vertigo. If this is your state, how do you overcome self?

› Record the answers to these questions in your personal journal: As you have asked and answered the application questions in this book, have you become more rooted and grounded in the natural laws and principles of primary greatness? Do you have a firmer grasp on the ultimate questions: *What are my life and work all about? What is really important here? What is my real worth? How am I doing in my journey toward primary greatness?*

A FINAL INTERVIEW WITH STEPHEN R. COVEY

In the twenty-five years since the publication of The 7 Habits, *Dr. Stephen R. Covey's Circle of Influence grew to encompass the entire globe. He consulted with kings and presidents, and taught millions of people through every imaginable channel the principles of effective living. By the time of his death in 2012, he had been named one of the most influential people in the world and* The 7 Habits *the most significant book on self-improvement in a century.*

He continued to teach the 7 Habits all his life. Additionally, the radically changing times called forth even deeper wisdom from Dr. Covey, some of which we'd like to share with you now.

The following is a synthesis of the responses Dr. Covey gave near the close of his life to vital questions he was often asked in interviews or during speeches. We have done our best to bring together his final thoughts in his own words into what might be considered his final interview. It can also be found in the 25th Anniversary Edition of The 7 Habits of Highly Effective People.

What has changed since *The 7 Habits* first appeared?

Change itself has changed. It's accelerated beyond anything any of us ever could have imagined. Technological revolutions seem to occur hourly. We grapple with economic uncertainty. Global power relations shift dramatically, sometimes overnight. And much of the world is terror-stricken, both psychologically and literally.

Our personal lives have radically changed too. The pace of life is now at light speed. We are connected to work 24/7. We used to try to do more with less; now many of us are trying to do everything at once.

But one thing hasn't changed and never will change—the only thing you can rely on—the fact that there are timeless and universal principles. They never change. They apply everywhere in the world at all times. Principles like fairness, honesty, respect, vision, accountability, and initiative govern our lives in the same way that natural laws, like gravity, dictate the consequences of falling off a building. If you go over the edge, you fall. It's a natural principle.

And that's why I am fundamentally optimistic. I am an optimist because I believe in changeless principles. I know that if we live by them, they will work for us.

Unlike a rock that falls if dropped from a building, we are capable of choosing whether to jump. We are not unconscious beings to be merely pulled or pushed around by impersonal forces. As humans, we are endowed with the gifts of conscience, imagination, self-awareness, and independent will. These are amazing gifts that animals do not possess. We can sense right from wrong. We can stand apart from ourselves and evaluate our own behavior. We can live out of our imagination, the future we wish to create, instead of being held hostage by the memory of our past. And the more we exercise these endowments, the greater becomes our freedom to choose. We can choose to make principles work for us or against us. I revel in that ability to choose.

To live with change, we need principles that don't change.

However, there's a problem. Too many of us—more than ever, I'm afraid—are trying to take a shortcut around the principles of life. We want love but not commitment. We want success without paying the price. We want thin bodies and our cake too. In other words, we want something we can never have—the rewards of good character without good character.

That's why I wrote *The 7 Habits of Highly Effective People*. I believe that our culture is drifting from its anchor in those principles, and I want to point to the consequences—that neglecting principles can only result in the shipwreck of our lives. In like manner, I promise you that, in the long run, if you will live in alignment with principles, you will prosper personally and professionally.

Are the 7 Habits still relevant?

I believe the 7 Habits are more relevant than ever.

No one has been more surprised, humbled, and thrilled by the influence of *The 7 Habits* than I have. I'm continually amazed at the effect the book has had on so many people in so many countries. I am so grateful that so many of my associates and friends have taken up the challenge to live and teach the habits.

Of course, I am just like everyone else who struggles to practice the 7 Habits every day. It's not easy, but it's a challenge. I have found it deeply inspiring to wake up each day and think through my mission in life and my important goals, and make small steps toward those things that are most meaningful. I have found it most difficult to live by Habit 5: Seek First to Understand, Then to Be Understood. I have worked at trying to become more patient and a better listener, and I think I have made some progress.

But I can tell you that living the 7 Habits is an exhilarating lifelong challenge. That's why I worry when people say they've read the book. I'm afraid they might see something in me that doesn't line up with what I've written. I'm also afraid they will think that reading the book makes them effective overnight—I hope people take seriously the message that you are never *done* with the 7 Habits.

I'm thrilled to see that more and more people around the world are being trained in the 7 *Habits* and that thousands have been certified to teach the 7 Habits inside their own organizations. People are attending 7 *Habits* classes online and in traditional classrooms in more than 140 countries. Even more exciting to me is that tens of thousands of schoolchildren are learning the 7 Habits. In some settings, entire corporations, government agencies, universities, and school systems have adopted the 7 Habits as an organizational philosophy and are finding great success with it.

Why do the 7 Habits continue to influence lives? I think it is because the 7 Habits help people identify their best selves and live accordingly. People, particularly the young, instinctively feel the power of the principles embodied in the 7 Habits and, deep down, they want more than shortcuts through life. People who lose themselves in the hyperactivity of the world want to regain control of their own destinies.

The 7 Habits give people their lives back. They get back the power to choose. They explore and discover their deepest, most cherished purposes. They gain the tools to create and control their own future.

We hear a lot today about identity theft. The greatest identity theft is not when someone takes your wallet or steals your credit card. The greater theft happens when we forget who we really are, when we begin to believe that our worth and identity come from how well we stack up compared to others, instead of recognizing that each of us has immeasurable worth and potential, independent of any comparison. This kind of theft comes from being immersed in a culture of shortcuts whereby people are unwilling to pay the price for true success. In our families, among friends, at work, we are constantly in the service of an artificial self-image. When man found the mirror, he began to lose his soul. He became more concerned with his image than with his true self; he became a product of the social mirror. His center of identity and worth moved outside of himself.

The 7 Habits bring you back to yourself. The 7 Habits remind you of your true nature. They remind you that *you* are in charge of your life. You are responsible—no one else—for your choices. No one outside yourself can make you think, do, or feel anything you do not choose for yourself. They remind you that you are the programmer and can write the program for your own future. They teach us that life is a team sport, and that interdependence, working cooperatively with others, is a higher state of being than independence.

Change is hard. How can I change?

I suggest two practices for making changes in your life. The first is to follow your conscience. I speak a lot about the idea that between stimulus (what happens to us) and response (what we do about it) is a space to choose, and what we do with that space ultimately determines our growth and happiness. In this space lie the four human endowments of conscience, imagination, self-awareness, and independent will. Of the four, conscience is the governing one. Often when we are not at peace in our lives, it is because we are living lives in violation of our conscience, and deep down, we know it. We can tap into conscience simply by asking ourselves questions and pausing to hear the answer. For example, try asking yourself the following questions: What is the most important thing I need to start doing in my personal life that would have the greatest positive impact? Think deeply. What comes to mind? Now ask yourself another question: What is the most important thing I need to start doing in my professional life that would have the greatest positive impact? Again, pause, think, and go deep inside yourself to find the answer. If you're like me, you'll recognize those most important things by listening to your conscience—that voice of wisdom, self-awareness, and common sense within you.

Another great question to ask yourself is: What is life now asking of me? Pause. Think carefully. You may sense that you've been unfocused and need to be far more careful with the way you spend your time. Or you may decide that you need to start eating better and exercising because you're constantly tired. Or you may sense that there is a key relationship you need to repair. Whatever it is, there is great strength and power in following through with a change that is endorsed by your conscience. Without deep conviction, you won't have the strength to follow through with your goals when the going gets tough. And conviction comes through conscience.

We all have three different lives: a public life, a private life, and an inner life. Our public life is what others observe. Our private life is what we do when we are alone. Our inner life is that place we go to when we really want to examine our motives and our deepest desires. I highly recommend developing this inner life. This is the place where our conscience can be most instructive because, while here, we are in the best frame of mind to listen.

A second key to change is to change your role. As I've always said, if you want to make incremental changes in your life, change your behaviors. However, if you want to make significant change, work on your paradigm—the way in which you see and interpret the world. And the best way to change your paradigm is to change your role. You may get promoted to be a new project manager at work. You may become a new mother or a new grandfather. You may take on a new community responsibility. Suddenly, your role has changed, and you see the world differently and better behaviors naturally flow out of the changed perspective.

Sometimes role changes are external events, such as a change in job responsibility. But other times we can change our role just by changing our mindset or our perception of a situation. Let's say, for example, that you are seen as a control freak at work and know that you need to start trusting others and letting go. Well, perhaps you could see yourself differently and redefine your role from one of supervisor to one of advisor. With that change of role, this mental shift, you would start to see yourself as an advisor to your team members who are empowered to make decisions and seek your counsel when doing so instead of being the one who has to own everything and constantly follow up.

I'm often asked: Which of the 7 Habits is the most important? My answer is: The most important habit is the one you are having the most difficult time living. Use your endowments of self-awareness and conscience to help you sense which habit you may need to focus on. Often the best way to change is to pick the one thing, the single habit, and make small commitments to yourself related to that habit and keep them. Little by little, your discipline and self-confidence will increase.

I see what the 7 Habits can do for me personally, but what if my company or organization doesn't practice the 7 Habits?
Everything starts with the individual, because all meaningful change comes from the inside out. When you start the personal process of change, you will soon find that you are also changing your environment as your influence expands and your example of integrity impresses others. Only after you have successfully begun working on yourself can you start working on the organization.

My great focus is to build the 7 Habits into the culture at large—to help us move on from the Industrial Age mindset of top-down command and control.

That Industrial Age is still with us mentally. It treats people as things to be controlled. It's the mindset that people are inter-changeable things, that one person is the same as another, when we all know that every person has unique gifts and is capable of making a contribution no one else can make. On financial state-ments, people are treated as expenses rather than as the highest-leveraged asset we have. Even if you're a benevolent autocrat, you're still controlling. This is the key flaw of most organizations today.

The 7 Habits can change all that. A 7 Habits culture is deeply empowering to everyone involved in it. In such a culture, every person has tremendous value. Complementary teams are care-fully designed to leverage the productive strengths of all team members and render their weaknesses irrelevant, as in a singing group where the alto doesn't try to take the place of the tenor or the soprano. All are needed. The key is to unleash them to find their own voices—to aim what they love to do and what they do well at the human needs they serve.

I am so humbled to see how the 7 Habits have helped trans-form teams and organizations around the world.

For instance, the 7 Habits are the creed of a great mining company in Mexico. Everyone from the CEO to the coal miner is trained in the 7 Habits. Everyone is valued. Productivity sky-rocketed while accident rates plunged as everyone took responsi-bility for results. Spouses started calling up the company asking, "What have you done with my husband or wife? They are com-pletely changed!" And now whole families are being trained.

I have learned that it takes more than great individuals to make a great company. An organization must also live by the 7 Habits *as an organization*. This means taking initiative, hav-ing a crystal-clear mission and strategy, consistently executing on priorities, thinking win-win with all stakeholders, and syner-gistically innovating for the future. Thinking within the frame-work of the 7 Habits is crucial to the success of any organization.

Building a 7 Habits culture is not just the CEO's job, it's everyone's job. In such a culture, all are leaders.

In the end, my passion has been to build principle-centered leadership into the culture of organizations everywhere. That kind of leadership is for everyone, not just the CEO. All true leadership is based on moral authority, not formal authority. Gandhi never held a formal position. Suu Kyi and Nelson Mandela gained their moral authority from years of imprisonment for the sake of conscience.

All my life, I've been a teacher. I've never held a position of high responsibility, but I've felt highly responsible for fulfilling my own mission. Anyone who takes the 7 Habits seriously becomes a leader.

You've always taught that people should think about the legacy they leave. What will be your legacy?

On a personal basis, I hope my greatest legacy is with my family, in their happiness and the quality of the lives they lead. Nothing has brought me more happiness and satisfaction than my family. It is what is most important to me. I agree with the observation of a wise leader who once said, "No success can compensate for failure in the home." Truly, the work you do within your own home is the greatest work you'll ever do. The family is of supreme importance and deserves more time and attention than we traditionally give it. People will spend hundreds of hours thinking through a detailed strategy at work, but won't bother to spend a few hours planning how to build a stronger family.

That said, I don't believe in the false dichotomy that to be successful at home, you have to less successful at work. It is not an either/or. With careful planning, you can do both. In fact, success in one will breed success in the other. Also, it is never too late to start anew with your family if you have neglected them in the past.

On a professional basis, when I'm asked what I want to be known for, my answer is simple: my work with children. I believe that every child is a leader and should be seen as such.

When it comes to children, don't define them by their behavior. Visualize and affirm them as leaders. Leadership is affirming people's worth and potential so clearly that they are inspired to see it in themselves.

We can raise a generation of leaders by teaching children their innate worth and goodness—by helping them see within themselves the great power and potential they have.

I am so pleased to see that thousands of schools around the world are now teaching the 7 Habits to children, teaching them who they really are and what they are capable of. We're teaching them integrity, resourcefulness, self-discipline, the win-win way of life. We're teaching them to welcome instead of distrust people who are different from them. We're teaching them how to Sharpen the Saw—to never stop growing and improving and learning.

This is being done through our *The Leader in Me* program that is being implemented in thousands of schools around the world. In these schools, children learn that everyone is a leader, not just a few popular ones. They learn the difference between primary success that comes from real, honest achievement and secondary success—worldly recognition—and they learn to value primary success. They learn that they have a marvelous gift of choice, that they don't have to be discouraged victims or cogs in a machine.

Imagine the future if children grow up deeply connected to these principles, banishing victimism and dependency, suspicion and defensiveness—as fully responsible citizens who take very seriously their obligations to others. That future is possible.

That's what I want to be remembered for.

What does the future hold for your body of work?

In my heart of hearts, I am a teacher. After completing my formal education, I became a professor, a job that I loved. As I began to detect my own mission, it became clear that this idea of principle-centered leadership, as embodied in *The 7 Habits* and my other works, was far bigger than I was. I knew that unless I built an organization to steward and institutionalize this message, its importance and relevance might fade after I was gone.

With that in mind, I decided to start a business, to build an organization that was devoted to spreading principle-centered leadership throughout the world. It started with Covey Leadership Center, which later merged with FranklinQuest to become FranklinCovey. The mission of our company is to enable greatness in people, organizations, and societies everywhere through the application of principle-centered leadership. We now operate in over 140 countries. I am proud of the mission, vision, values, and performance of the organization. It is doing exactly what I hoped it would do. Perhaps most important, FranklinCovey is not dependent upon me whatsoever, and will continue this work long after I am gone.

You have said that your most important final message is to live life in crescendo. What does that mean?

It means that the most important work you will ever do is always ahead of you. It is never behind you. You should always be expanding and deepening your commitment to that work. Retirement is a false concept. You may retire from a job, but never retire from meaningful projects and contributions.

Crescendo is a musical term. It means to play music with ever greater energy and volume, with strength and striving. The opposite is *diminuendo*, which means to lower the volume, to back off, to play it safe, to become passive, to whimper away your life.

So live life in crescendo. It's essential to live with that thought. Regardless of what you have or haven't accomplished, you have important contributions to make. Avoid the temptation to keep looking in the rearview mirror at what you have done and instead look ahead with optimism. I am excited about my forthcoming book *Life in Crescendo*, which I am writing with my daughter Cynthia.

No matter what your age or position in life, if you live by the 7 Habits, you are never finished contributing. You are always seeking something higher and better from life: the next fascinating challenge, greater understanding, more intense romance, more meaningful love. You may get satisfaction from past accomplishments, but the next great contribution is always on the horizon. You have relationships to build, a community to serve, a family to strengthen, problems to solve, knowledge to gain, and great works to create.

One of my daughters asked me if I had finished impacting the world when I wrote *The 7 Habits of Highly Effective People*. I think I startled her with my answer: This is not to overvalue myself, but I truly *believe* that my best work is ahead of me.

Stephen R. Covey died July 16, 2012, at the age of seventy-nine, still fully engaged in about ten different writing projects. He never retired in the traditional sense, but lived in crescendo right up to the end. As the influence of his thinking continues to spread around the world at an ever faster rate, transforming the lives of schoolchildren and executives and ordinary people everywhere, we believe with him that his best work is still ahead of him.

ENDNOTES

1. http://usatoday30.usatoday.com/news/nation/story/2012-04-07/titanic-rearrange-deck-chairs/54084648/1.

2. Walter Lord, *A Night to Remember*, Holt Paperbacks, 2004, 36

3. Stephen R. Covey, *The 7 Habits of Highly Effective People*, Simon & Schuster, 2013, 22.

4. Jessica Lahey, "The Benefits of Character Education," *The Atlantic*, May 6, 2013. http://www.theatlantic.com/national/archive/2013/05/the-benefits-of-character-education/275585/.

5. Paul Tough, *How Children Succeed*, Houghton Mifflin Harcourt, 2013, xix.

6. See N.E. Ruedy, F. Gino, C. Moore, M.E. Schweitzer, "The Cheater's High: The Unexpected Affective Benefits of Unethical Behavior," *Journal of Personality and Social Psychology*, 2013, vol. 105, no. 4, 531–548.

7. Christopher Peterson, Martin Seligman, *Character Strengths and Virtues: A Handbook and Classification*, Oxford University Press, 2004, 5.

8. *The 7 Habits*, 43.

9. Charles E. Hummel, *The Tyranny of the Urgent*, IVP Books, 1994, 6.

10. Benjamin Franklin, *Autobiography*, Houghton-Mifflin, 1896, 113.

11. Albert E. Gray, "The Common Denominator of Success,"

http://www.kordellnorton.com/Nort%20Notes/Nort%20 Notes%20-%20Common_Denominator%20by%20Gray .htm.

12. Marianne Williamson, *A Return to Love: Reflections on the Principles of "A Course in Miracles,"* HarperOne, 1996, 190.

INDEX

ABOUT THE AUTHOR

Stephen R. Covey was an internationally respected leadership authority, family expert, teacher, organizational consultant, and author who dedicated his life to teaching principle-centered living and leadership to build both families and organizations. He earned an M.B.A. from Harvard University and a doctorate from Brigham Young University, where he was a professor of organizational behavior and business management and also served as director of university relations and assistant to the president.

Dr. Covey was the author of several acclaimed books, including the international bestseller *The 7 Habits of Highly Effective People*, which was named the #1 Most Influential Business Book of the Twentieth Century and one of the top-ten most influential management books ever. It has sold more than 20 million copies in thirty-eight languages throughout the world. Other bestsellers include *First Things First, Principle-Centered Leadership,* and *The 7 Habits of Highly Effective Families*, bringing the combined total to more than 25 million books sold.

As a father of nine and grandfather of forty-three, he received the 2003 Fatherhood Award from the National Fatherhood Initiative, which he said was the most meaningful award he ever received. Other awards given to Dr. Covey include the Thomas More College Medallion for continuing service to humanity, Speaker of the Year in 1999, the Sikh's 1998 International Man of Peace Award, the 1994 International Entrepreneur of the Year Award, and the National Entrepreneur of the Year Lifetime Achievement Award for Entrepreneurial Leadership. Dr. Covey was recognized as one of *Time* magazine's 25 Most Influential Americans and received seven honorary doctorate degrees.

Dr. Covey was the cofounder and vice chairman of Franklin-Covey Company, the leading global professional services firm, with offices in 123 countries. They share Dr. Covey's vision, discipline, and passion to inspire, lift, and provide tools for change and growth of individuals and organizations throughout the world.

Franklin Covey Co. (NYSE: FC) is global company specializing in performance improvement. We help organizations achieve results that require a change in human behavior. Our expertise is in seven areas: leadership, execution, productivity, trust, sales performance, customer loyalty, and education. Franklin Covey clients have included 90 percent of the Fortune 100, more than 75 percent of the Fortune 500, thousands of small- and mid-sized businesses, as well as numerous government entities and educational institutions. Franklin Covey has more than forty direct and licensee offices providing professional services in over 150 countries.

For more information, visit www.franklincovey.com

THE ULTIMATE COMPETITIVE ADVANTAGE

FranklinCovey is a global company specializing in performance improvement. We help organizations achieve results that require a change in human behavior.

Our expertise is in seven areas:

LEADERSHIP

Develops highly effective leaders who engage others to achieve results.

EXECUTION

Enables organizations to execute strategies that require a change in human behavior.

PRODUCTIVITY

Equips people to make high-value choices and execute with excellence in the midst of competing priorities.

TRUST

Builds a high-trust culture of collaboration and engagement, resulting in greater speed and lower costs.

SALES PERFORMANCE

Transforms the buyer-seller relationship by helping clients succeed.

CUSTOMER LOYALTY

Drives faster growth and improves frontline performance with accurate customer- and employee-loyalty data.

EDUCATION

Helps schools transform their performance by unleashing the greatness in every educator and student.

LEARN MORE

Want to learn more about how to dramatically improve the effectiveness of not just individuals, but your organization? Visit **www.franklincovey.com**.

Buy the #1 *Wall Street Journal* Bestseller

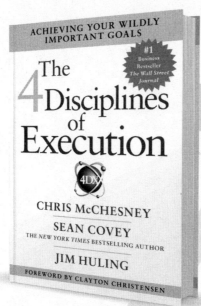

Executing on the goals that require the hearts and minds of your people!

"In place of the top-down, control-oriented management techniques of the industrial age, the 4 Disciplines offer a release-oriented, knowledge-worker-age approach to executing goals and strategies, an approach that engages people's hearts and minds towards a common goal unlike anything I've ever seen. Truly a profound work!"

Stephen R. Covey, author of *The 7 Habits of Highly Effective People*

For more information visit www.4dxbook.com